TRIX

OF THE GRADE

Tutor A and Tutor B

Gower

Published by
Gower Publishing Limited
Gower House
Croft Road
Aldershot
Hampshire GU11 3HR
England

Gower
Old Post Road
Brookfield
Vermont 05036
USA

Reprinted 1996

Tutor A and Tutor B have asserted their right under the Copyright, Design and Patents Act 1988 to be identified as the author of this work.

British Library Cataloguing in Publication Data

Trix of the grade
    1. Grading and marking (Students)
    2. Educational tests and measurements
    378.1'672

ISBN 0 566 07804 X

Typeset in Trade Gothic by FdK Design Consultants, Dorking and printed in Great Britain by The University Press, Cambridge.

CONTENTS

List of figures

PREFACE

If you are a student in higher education you may want to work hard and get excellent grades, or you may just want decent grades in return for a small amount of effort. In either case this book will help.

Most students go through higher education with little or no idea of why they get the grades they do or what they can do to change them. They think that marking is a mysterious process which they are unable to influence. *Trix of the Grade* blows the lid off the 'marking myth'. In plain language it will teach you a series of clever 'Trix' and help you get the best grades possible.

Trix of the Grade tells you how lecturers really mark work and why they give high grades. We are highly qualified lecturers but have not revealed our identities because this book contains a lot of 'inside information' which wouldn't normally be available to students. We are also experienced business consultants and use many of these 'Trix' out there in the 'real world'.

Higher education, like all human activity, is partly a game. To play the game well you need to know the rules and learn some of the 'set plays'. The 'Trix' we talk about aren't ways of cheating. They are practical guidelines that will improve your performance. Using this book you can learn the game in just a couple of hours. You can then use it as a reference for specific situations – read the relevant parts and use the 'Trix' and 'Examples' you find to get the grades you want.

We have used Business Studies as an example, but most of the 'Trix' are the same no matter what course you are taking and no matter what job you want at the end of it.

Good reading and good luck!

1 WHAT IS HIGHER EDUCATION?

Before you can learn how to maximize your performance in HE (Higher Education) you need to understand exactly what HE is. HE used to be about *knowledge.* It was a system in which a small number of privileged people were able to study, quite literally, at the feet of the masters of knowledge. We make no apologies for the sexist language – that's how it was. Most of this knowledge had little or no practical use, but there you go!

Most modern subjects require students to acquire a great deal of knowledge before they are allowed to practise their profession in the real world, the obvious examples being science, medicine, law and engineering. But most graduates aren't employed for their knowledge; they are employed because they have demonstrated an ability to learn and to solve problems for their employers. Of course, one popular method of demonstrating these abilities is to achieve good grades.

Many students go to university or college believing that they are entering a bigger school to learn more difficult things. But HE is not like school – it's very different. Let's take a look at those differences now.

There is an old adage that says 'He who pays the piper calls the tune'. This applies to both schools and HE institutions. In other words, they do what they are paid to do. The funding of the UK education system is a very complex and rather tedious subject that we won't spend much time discussing, but it's worth noting a few important facts.

Schools are paid by local and central government to teach pupils. Specifically, they are paid to teach pupils how to pass exams. Indeed, league tables of exam results are published to tell parents how well a school fulfils this task. On the other hand, HE institutions are paid to undertake various activities of which teaching is only one. While the government does indeed give money to HE institutions for teaching students, they also give them a great deal of money to carry out research on behalf of the nation. Nor is the government the only source of funding for HE institutions; they also gain income from the private sector which pays them to undertake specific research projects and teach specialized courses.

So, as you can see, HE institutions aren't just there to teach students. From your point of view the story gets even worse. Because the amount of money given by the government for teaching students is constantly decreasing, HE institutions are putting more and more effort into research and generating income from the private sector. This is why you will find that the ratio of tutors to students is getting worse all the time – HE institutions are trying to teach increasing numbers of students with ever diminishing funds.

2 DEALING WITH TUTORS

Tutors aren't just clever teachers – they are very different animals. Let's find out exactly what they are.

WHAT DO TUTORS DO?

It's fairly easy to see what a schoolteacher is employed to do – teach pupils. Included in a schoolteacher's job are a number of other responsibilities such as marking, attending meetings and maybe running a club or two, but essentially they are paid to teach.

As you will probably have gathered by now, tutors aren't paid just to teach. Usually their contracts demand that they also do a certain amount of research and work for the private sector. Not only are tutors required to undertake these other activities, many of them much prefer them and may see teaching as an unwelcome intrusion into their time! Another point to bear in mind is that, unlike schoolteachers, tutors quite often have more than one job. Many of them also earn money by writing books and consulting in the private sector.

Schoolteachers tend to work fairly regular hours. But tutors, like students, have no fixed hours of work and don't attend their HE institutions all the time. Many of their activities take place outside their HE institution.

In summary, you can see that a tutor's principal loyalty may not be towards your education. Indeed it may be quite low on their list of priorities. To the student a tutor's life is like an iceberg – four-fifths invisible. Don't, however, let this depress you; after all, everyone is in the same situation and in this book we will tell you how to make the best of it.

Why were they employed?

Schoolteachers are generally professionals. Nearly all UK teaching posts require a teaching qualification, and would-be teachers have to successfully complete a long course of teaching practice before they qualify. Teachers are employed because they can teach; they don't have to be experts in their subjects.

The opposite is true of tutors. Tutors are employed because they are experts in their subject area. Depending on the particular HE institution concerned, teaching ability will have had little or no importance at their job interview. Most HE tutors have no teaching qualifications and are subject to little or no testing to measure how effective they are at the task!

Of course, some tutors are excellent teachers. They are easy to identify by the fact that they seem interested in what they are doing and you can understand what they are talking about – at least some of the time! Other tutors, although highly qualified within their subject, are very poor teachers and struggle to convey any of their knowledge effectively. In general you can expect HE tutors to be less effective teachers than their counterparts in schools.

What will they teach you?

What you were taught at school was almost certainly more or less the same as other pupils at other schools, because your teachers will have worked within tight guidelines issued by senior education specialists. Most of these guidelines are set out in the National Curriculum.

On the other hand, tutors can teach you more or less what they want. Two tutors covering the same subject at the same HE institution might teach you quite different things. They might even contradict each other. Far from being frowned upon, this is often encouraged in HE because it exposes you to a range of expert opinions from which you can draw your own conclusions. You might consider this confusing but, as one of the aims of HE is to develop your judgement, from a tutor's point of view it's reasonable!

How do they teach you?

Most school teaching takes place under the close supervision of a teacher. It usually starts with some sort of input from the teacher in the form of facts or an explanation of a concept. Then typically you are given an exercise which allows you to practise using these facts or concepts.

On the other hand, tutors use a wide range of teaching methods including:

- talking and presenting to you (lectures)
- having conversations with you in small groups (tutorials)
- encouraging you to learn from other students (group work)
- encouraging you to learn on your own (research)

Of course you could say that schoolteachers use all these techniques as well, and to a certain extent that's true. It's a question of balance. Tutors will expect you to learn far more from activities such as group work and research than schoolteachers. In HE circles this is known as learning facilitation or action learning, and is very popular at the moment.

There is a trend among some tutors to take this concept still further by employing a technique known as open learning. This means that they don't set out to actively teach you anything at all, but just give you a few hints on how to find things out on your own on the grounds that you are more likely to remember things you have discovered yourself. Well that's certainly true, and you will find *Trix of the Grade* of great help with such activities.

Parents, teachers and tutors

Schoolteachers act *in loco parentis* – literally, 'in place of the parent'. While you were at school they undertook some of the responsibilities of your parent(s) or guardian(s). They had an obligation to see that you behaved in a disciplined way and that you benefited from your time at school. They will have taken steps to ensure that you did what was ultimately in your best interests. In practical terms this might have meant putting you in detention if you didn't hand your homework in on time or misbehaved in class.

Tutors don't have any such parental responsibilities. If you are in an HE institution you will be treated as an adult. Tutors only have to see you at scheduled times and mark your work. They don't have to ensure that you attend lectures or tutorials and they don't have to ensure that you hand work in on time – if you hand in work late they might simply fail it. If you don't attend a lecture or tutorial they might not even notice you weren't there – attendance is not usually compulsory. If you miss some lectures or tutorials they probably won't help you to catch up! In short, tutors aren't responsible for your learning – you are.

Judge and jury

If you have only recently left school you will probably have experienced continuous assessment. This is where your teacher marks particular pieces of work, and these marks count towards the grade you get for your qualification. However, since continuous assessment is nearly always combined with traditional exams which are marked by external examiners, your teachers will have had little or no direct influence on your grades. In other words, schoolteachers teach, and someone else does the marking.

In HE institutions most of your work will be marked by those tutors who are teaching you. Of course, their marking is sometimes cross-checked by other tutors and external examiners but, for all practical purposes, you can consider them as your judge and jury.

THE DOS AND DON'TS

Before we explore the dos and dont's of dealing with tutors let's recall some sobering facts:

- Tutors aren't responsible for you or your learning.
- Teaching might not be their highest priority.
- Tutors can be difficult to track down.
- Tutors have a great deal of influence over your grades.

Now let's also summarize some of the more distressing possibilities:

- Some tutors might not care whether or not you learn.
- Some tutors might actively avoid teaching at all costs.
- Some tutors might actively avoid students!

It's wise to assume that, unless you do something to change the status quo, many tutors will be, at best, indifferent to you. So is it worth making the extra effort to get on well with tutors? – Yes. Tutors are like all people; they have likes and dislikes and are not emotionless robots. These likes and dislikes could prove very important to your future. Consider this.

At the end of your course your tutors will sit on something known as an award board – a highly confidential meeting at which your final grade is determined. The decision reached by this board is more or less set in stone, since you are unlikely to have any effective means of appealing against it, or even of finding out what was said about you.

Suppose that your marks place you on the borderline between two classifications. The tutors will spend some time discussing your case and will then decide to put you 'up' or 'down'. In order to make this decision they will go through something like the following process.

First they will consider any mitigating circumstance which may have had an adverse effect on your performance. Next they will assess your performance in what are known as 'indicative areas'. These are elements of your course which the senior tutors and external examiners have decided are a good indication of a student's overall ability. You may or may not be told what these elements are, but in general they are individual projects – particularly final-year projects. After this they might look for something termed 'progression' – that is evidence that your grades have, on the whole, improved throughout the course.

If at the end of this process there is no compelling reason to either upgrade or downgrade you the decision will depend on how well you are liked or disliked by the tutors. One scenario is that a tutor who particularly dislikes you says something like 'We must ensure that academic standards are maintained. I can't see any reason to put him up', and you would probably go down. Conversely, if you are well liked by most of the tutors one of them will say something like 'I think he is a great student; he was well motivated and committed to the course. He helped us out in induction week as well'. As long as most of the tutors share this view it is almost certain that you would go up. Naturally, none of the tutors will mention liking or disliking you and will certainly deny any bias if asked. Nevertheless, this will be the determining factor.

As you can see, if you deliberately upset tutors you either don't care about your education or you are very stupid. However, it's quite easy to annoy tutors in ways you might not have considered. For example, saying something like 'I don't think I will get a good grade in this subject because I find it boring' is guaranteed to create a bad impression.

If you find a subject difficult or boring, say something like 'I find this subject difficult and I hope you will be patient with me if I ask silly questions'. The tutor will be flattered. You are telling them that something they are good at is difficult. This is likely to make them more helpful and lenient.

Despite all that we have said, most tutors are conscientious and professional in their dealings with students. In particular they nearly always set out to:

- give you everything you need to complete their course
- treat all students fairly and equally
- give honest answers to sensible questions
- help you when you have a problem

So let's take a closer look at what you can do to get the best grades from your tutors.

Pay attention

If you pay attention to tutors they won't have to repeat information they gave earlier. This happens continuously in school and generally results in the guilty pupil being reprimanded for not listening. Tutors aren't allowed to tell students off, but it doesn't stop them thinking you are a wally all the same.

Read the documentation

Make sure you read all the documentation you are given. This will probably have taken the tutor a long time to prepare and have been specifically designed to answer common questions. If you ask a question that's answered in such documentation the tutor will think you are either too lazy or too stupid to read it.

Don't allege 'bad marking'

Never accuse tutors of bad marking. If you think you deserve a higher grade raise the issue in a calm, non-confrontational way.

In these situations it is important not to compare your grade with another student's. If, for example, you say to a tutor 'I did the same as my friend and she got an 'A', why have I only got a 'C'?', you are effectively alleging that the tutor is being unfair. Such a comment is likely to result in a response such as 'If you did the same as your friend, surely that's cheating and I might have to investigate you both for collusion'! Even if you genuinely believe that the tutor has been unfair you must never say, or even imply, this.

In virtually all HE institutions you have the right to formally appeal against a grade. This involves having your work marked by a second tutor. If you are ever tempted to do this, bear in mind the following. First, in most appeal procedures it's possible for your grade to be put down as well as up. Second, most tutors are very keen on something called collegiality, which means that they will generally go out of their way to watch each other's backs. Therefore, the second marker of your work is quite likely to be the original marker's friend or close professional colleague and will probably bend over backwards to ensure that they give you the same grade. Third, if you 'win' the appeal you won't be very popular with the tutor. This might result in you winning the battle but losing the war!

If you want a higher grade for some work that has already been marked and you think that you really deserve it, don't threaten the tutor with an appeal. While most tutors are certainly keen to avoid appeals on account of the extra work and aggravation, saying something like 'If you don't give me a better grade I will appeal' will probably have a very negative effect. Nobody likes being threatened and, even if the tutor thinks you have a point, they are unlikely to increase your grade after such a comment. Furthermore, if you do end up going to appeal, the tutor will almost certainly refer to any such threatening comments. This will not help your case at all.

If you are unhappy with a grade make an appointment to see the tutor. During the meeting go out of your way to be extremely polite and flattering, but don't be sycophantic. Say to the tutor something like 'I'm struggling a little bit here, perhaps you can help. I put a lot of effort into this assignment and I'm very disappointed with the grade. Can you tell me where I went wrong please?' The tutor will then happily go through your work with you.

Listen carefully, and with an open mind, to what the tutor says and don't take the tutor's comments personally. After this, you may find that you agree with the original grade. This does not mean that the exercise has been a waste of time – far from it. You will have probably picked up valuable information which you can use to good effect in future assignments.

Alternatively, you may find that, after going through your work, the tutor says something like 'Having spoken to you I see some evidence of a deeper understanding, so I think I can increase your grade a little.' However, this is not likely and you can expect any increase to be quite small. If no increase is volunteered and you genuinely believe that you have been harshly marked say something like 'I very much respect your opinion, and the last thing I want to do is upset you. I hope you won't be offended if I ask you to show my work to another tutor for their comments'. Leave the assignment with the tutor and make another appointment to collect it at a later date.

If your grade does go up, **never** tell other students and, even more importantly, don't boast about it. One of the key reasons that tutors hate changing grades is that they don't want all the students to start challenging them since that would involve them in hours of extra work and much aggravation. If tutors find out that you have, albeit inadvertently, encouraged other students to query their marking you will be very unpopular!

Don't show off

Only ask questions when you really need to. Don't ask questions to show off in front of the class. Similarly don't try to outdo or undermine the tutor in order to impress your friends – the tutor will win in the end!

Don't hassle them

Only speak to tutors in the normal teaching sessions or when you have made an appointment. Don't grab them in corridors and, above all, don't talk shop to them if you happen to encounter them in a pub.

Tutors can be great allies or difficult adversaries. You would be amazed at how much red tape they can use to hinder you and, in a large building with numerous places to hide, they can become extremely elusive! Of course, there are appeal procedures, complaints procedures and student charters to fall back on if you have to. But our advice is make friends with them and stay friends.

3 LEARNING TO LEARN

Believe it or not, you actually have to learn how to study. We all have strengths and weaknesses relating to our personalities, characters and cognitive style (more of which later). There is no universal answer to the question of 'how to study'. What is good for one of your friends may not be good for you. Finding and developing your own study style is the key.

WHAT IS THERE TO LEARN?

Most students underperform in HE because they think tutors will be testing their *knowledge* of a subject. This is not surprising since this was nearly always the case when they were at school. Doing well in school exams depends on being able to recall knowledge almost 'parrot fashion'. But teaching and learning in HE is much more complex. It follows a sequence of 'levels'. Here they are, in ascending order:

1. skills and knowledge

2. analysis

3. understanding

4. judgement

5. application

6. synthesis

As you progress through this sequence the learning becomes more and more difficult. And, as you would expect, the value of what you have learned increases. This sequence may run through a single subject or underlie your whole course.

Skills and knowledge

You might think of *skills* as having more to do with training than education. You are also quite likely to associate the acquisition of skills with physical, rather than mental, activities. For instance, you might say that a professional footballer has excellent skills associated with ball control. Likewise, you might think that a carpenter has good woodworking skills. In fact, the term 'skills' applies to mental as well as physical activities. Adding up simple numbers in your head is a skill you will probably have learned some time ago.

Skills are about mastering techniques and processes. Some skills you either possess or you don't. For example, if you are a car mechanic you can either replace the engine in a Ford Escort or you can't. With other skills, like playing football, there is no concept of ability or inability. It's a matter of degree. The question here is, how well do you play football? You will see why it's important to make this distinction a little later.

We have deliberately grouped skills and knowledge together because they are closely related. *Knowledge* relates to the learning of facts rather than techniques.

To learn skills and knowledge you have to memorize techniques and facts. This is generally regarded as the most basic form of learning. That's why people who trained at a technical college aren't usually paid as well as HE graduates. In our society only those with exceptional skills or knowledge, such as international sportspeople or master craftsmen, are regarded and rewarded highly.

Skills and knowledge are the basis for all other levels of learning, but don't think that they are easy to acquire – they are not.

Analysis

Analysis is very important for HE students. Later in this book we will be using analysis techniques to help you answer assignment and exam questions. To analyse something is to break it down into its component parts. In HE you will be asked to analyse case studies, books, essays and reports all the time. You will be taught various analysis techniques on your course and be expected to use them.

Tutors will generally be impressed by your ability to perform analysis, so it's worth getting good at it.

Use the analysis tools that your tutors like best. If you don't know what they are, ask them.

You need to analyse problems or situations so that you can answer questions such as 'Where are we?, and What do we know?'. Think of this in terms of everyday events.

An orienteer needs to decide which way to go by using a compass and map to analyse their position. They will first orient themselves using the compass and then ask questions such as:

- What can I see from here?
- Are there any special landmarks?
- Where did I set out?
- How long have I been going?

while using the map for guidance.

The analysis tools taught to you by your tutors are like the map and compass – especially the map. Of course, you need to decide which map to use, but more of that later. The following example shows what we mean.

In a tutorial you are asked to analyse the competitive position of a company in a case study. Your tutor tells you to use 'Porter's model for competition'. This model shows that competitive position is dependent on the five following factors:

- What other companies are in the market?
- Who are the company's customers?
- Who are the company's suppliers?
- Is there any threat of new companies entering the market?
- Is there any threat of substitute products to those supplied by the company becoming available?

A sensible use of this 'map' during the tutorial would be to look at the case study and try to answer each of these questions, writing your results down under the appropriate heading.

Understanding

Understanding is related to knowledge. You understand something when you know more than just the facts. You might be able to memorize this book word for word *(knowledge)*. You might even have worked out that it's been written using a lot of short sentences *(analysis)*. But if you don't *understand* what it's saying it's useless to you.

Judgement

The judge and jury in a law court decide who is telling the truth and who is not. They also decide what sentences are appropriate for those found guilty of a crime. The significance is that they make decisions. They come to conclusions about what is right and what is wrong. Of course, in reality, things aren't usually so clear-cut, and a court's job usually involves deciding to what extent something or someone is right. These *judgements* are based on their *understanding* and *analysis* of the facts. But courts can't make decisions arbitrarily; they can't find someone guilty because they don't like the look of them or are in a bad mood. They have to explain the reasoning behind their decision-making.

The situation for students in HE is much the same. If a question is testing your judgement, the conclusions you reach in your answer aren't as important as the process you used to reach them. Tutors will look for evidence that you have understood the relevant facts and gone through a logical decision-making process. Indeed, you might even reach conclusions with which the tutor disagrees but still be awarded a good grade because you have demonstrated that you have reached them in the correct way.

Application

Application is the ability to make use of *knowledge, analysis, understanding* and *judgement* in a practical way – in other words, to make use of what you have learned. As a student you will need to be able to apply what you have learned in order to solve problems presented to you in assignments and exam questions.

The purpose of teaching you to apply your learning is to simulate the real world of work. A good tutor will pose problems that relate directly to the types of task that employers might ask you to carry out. For example, if at the end of your course, you tell a prospective employer that you have learned to use a spreadsheet, they might ask 'What did your spreadsheets do?'. Questions like these are designed to find out whether or not you can *apply* what you have learned in a practical situation.

When speaking to potential employers, perhaps in an interview, make sure you tell them that you can apply what you have learned to practical problems. For example saying, 'I developed a spreadsheet which forecasts cash flow' sounds more practical and relevant than 'I learned to use a spreadsheet.'

Synthesis

Synthesis is the opposite of analysis. It's the assembly of component parts into a whole. The idea is that you put two and two together to make five. Synthesis is the ability to use *knowledge, understanding, judgement* and *application* to create something new and original. For example, we have used our experience in HE, business and writing to synthesize this book.

Here's an example that may be more relevant to you. Suppose in an assignment you are asked the following question:

Prepare a 2500 word report defining the countries that Clever Co. PLC should target in its forthcoming export drive *(see case study)*.

You probably wouldn't be able to answer this question without examining the individual areas of marketing, finance, operations, personnel, IT (Information Technology) and so on. You would then have to combine this research in a synthesized solution to the problem.

HOW TO REMEMBER

You might think that you have a bad memory, but have you? Our memories have different dimensions. Do you mean that you have a bad memory for recalling knowledge or is it skills that you have difficulty with?

Remembering knowledge can be difficult because much of it is abstract – it doesn't relate to daily life. To recall knowledge easily you need to associate it with something familiar.

Use a mnemonic. For example, the main classes of stars are given letters in a particular sequence by astronomers – O, B, A, F, G, K, M, R, N, S. Remembering this abstract sequence is difficult but 'Oh Be A Fine Girl, Kiss Me Right Now – Smack!' is not so hard.

Mastering skills requires a different strategy; you are much more likely to remember how to do something if you do it for yourself. For instance, if you are a business studies student trying to understand the discounted cash flow formula, you should do the calculations on several examples, rather than just try to remember it.

If you like to miss the odd session, try not to miss the practical ones like lab exercises. You will probably find that, minute for minute, they are more valuable than lectures and ordinary tutorials.

If your course uses a great deal of continuous assessment and open book exams, you might think that training your memory is a waste of time. However, having a good memory is useful, and everyone's memory will improve with practice.

HOW TO UNDERSTAND

Some students complain of a mental block when it comes to understanding certain concepts. For instance, many business studies students find numeric subjects difficult to master. They often make comments such as 'This is too difficult for me, and anyway the tutor hasn't explained it clearly enough'. They are implying that the problem resides with the tutor and not them. Not so. The student is the learner and is the one who needs to make the effort.

Mental blocks

Mental blocks are the result of a vicious circle. You find something difficult so you become demotivated. Because you are demotivated the learning becomes harder and so on. In order to break out of this circle you must first remember that there is nothing wrong with finding something hard. There is not even anything wrong in never being able to understand certain concepts very well at all. We aren't all Einsteins, so we might find grasping the theory of relativity a little tricky!

You are not likely to sail through HE finding everything easy – it's designed to be hard work! But don't worry, most HE courses are intended to be accessible so that you can apply certain knowledge without necessarily understanding it. For instance, you might not understand the mathematical principle that underlies the discounted cash flow formula. But, as long as you know about it, can remember it, and are able to apply it correctly, you will be in good shape.

Ask tutors to explain the *application* of things that you don't understand.

HOW TO ORGANIZE

Organizing is not the same as remembering. We all organize knowledge differently, because we have different cognitive styles that affect our ability to learn under particular circumstances. So what are these cognitive styles? Cognition is the process whereby we translate our sensory impressions (sound, sight, touch, smell and taste) into mental representations. It's important to realize that nobody understands this process fully. Researchers have only succeeded in understanding some of its practicalities.

Some people are imagers; they depend upon visual representations for organizing knowledge. These people can quickly and easily take on board information represented in pictures and diagrams. As you would expect, they also tend to use graphs and pictures when describing things to others. Other people are verbalizers; they are more comfortable with verbal and written information. They rarely use pictures or graphs intuitively, but express themselves powerfully with language.

If you don't know already, try to decide if you are an imager or a verbalizer.

Suppose you have a cube. The cube is then sliced into halves, then quarters, then eighths. Now answer this question: 'What does the cube look like?'.

It's likely that you will have assumed this puzzle would end with a question relating to the size, shape or number of the pieces of the cube. You will have been trying to organize this in your mind as you sliced up the cube. If you did this by developing an image of the cube in your mind you are an imager. If you only used the written instructions you are a verbalizer.

Here are some tools that might help you to organize knowledge. The tools that attract you will probably be the ones that best match your cognitive style.

Knowledge trees

Because academics like to classify things, much of the knowledge taught in HE can be fitted into a tree structure. For example, the Dewey decimal system used in most academic libraries is based on a tree structure. In more practical terms, if we want to understand how a car works we would probably start by breaking it down into assemblies and sub-assemblies until we get to the individual components (see Figure 3.1).

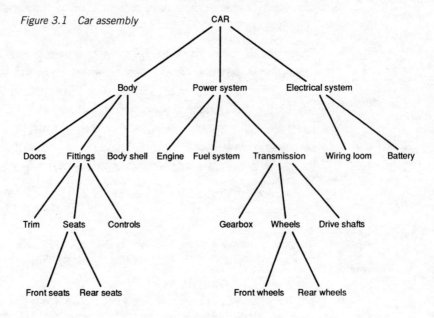

Figure 3.1   Car assembly

Many tutors present their lectures and other material in a tree structure, particularly if it's based on a textbook.

When you are at a lecture, try to draw a knowledge tree that represents the information being presented to you. This will help you both absorb the information at the time and revise it in the future.

Mind maps

Mind maps are more complex than knowledge trees. They are graphical devices for illustrating the relationships between various pieces of information in a way that echoes the way your mind works. They not only describe how information is related but are also capable of describing trains of thought. Figure 3.2 shows the mind map we used to organize this section of the book. Notice that not everything you might expect appears on the map. This is because mind maps don't necessarily store the information itself, they store the 'signposts' to it.

Figure 3.2   Mind map

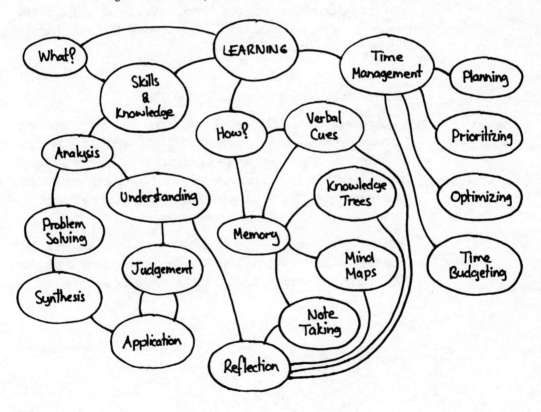

So how can you use mind maps for learning? You can sketch out maps that relate to knowledge presented in things like lectures and books. With mind maps you don't have to copy the method of organization used by the lecturer or author; you organize things in a way that makes sense to you. This is much more powerful than ordinary note-taking because you:

- relate the knowledge to what you already know
- relate the knowledge to things not directly connected to the specific subject
- actively process the knowledge instead of passively receiving it
- form a mental representation of the knowledge in your mind

You can change or even redraw mind maps as your understanding grows. In time, the maps which you use most frequently become committed to memory.

Verbal cues

Earlier (page 19) we talked about using mnemonics for remembering knowledge. Verbal cues are a similar technique for organizing knowledge. You can often organize knowledge by relating it to apparently unrelated things like images, phrases or pieces of music. For example, some people immediately conjure up an image of an apple falling on Sir Isaac Newton's head whenever the word 'gravity' is mentioned.

There are many ways of setting up verbal cues, but most experts would suggest linking information to cues that have high emotional impact for you. Things that make you laugh or feel like crying are a good idea.

A bolometer is a scientific instrument invented by a person called Langley. But what's it used for? Let's take a look at this verse from the book *A Random Walk in Science*.

> Oh Langley devised the bolometer
> It's really a kind of thermometer
> Which measures the heat
> From a polar bear's feet
> At a distance of half a kilometre

There is a quite a lot of information represented in this short verse. We now know that a bolometer:

- was invented by Langley

- measures temperature

- can measure temperature form a long distance away

- can measure very small differences in temperature

Let's take an example related to business studies. SWOT is an acronym for Strengths, Weaknesses, Opportunities, Threats. Here's the verbal cue for it. SWOT is linked in most people's minds with the word 'swat', meaning to destroy an insect. Swatting is a rapid activity for getting rid of flies and other insects when they become a problem. It therefore follows that a SWOT analysis is a fast technique for problem solving. This not only helps you to remember that SWOT analyses exist at all, but also what they are used for and how they work.

Try to relate acronyms to words that tell you something about the way in which the principles involved are applied.

Taking notes

In an ideal world all your tutors would give you comprehensive notes of all their lectures, but this is not an ideal world. Tutors don't always hand out notes. This is usually for one of three reasons. First, your HE institution might be trying to reduce its photocopying bill! Second, some tutors don't have the time or inclination to prepare them. Third, lecture material usually belongs to tutors – they have intellectual copyright over it – and they don't have to give you their notes if they don't want to.

So, given that you aren't likely to be given handouts all the time, what's the best way of taking notes? You might think you need to write down everything you see and hear during lectures. This is a bad idea for two reasons. First, you will find it almost impossible to write fast enough to keep up with the lecturer. Second, whilst you are writing you are not absorbing or *understanding* the lecture.

You might think that, by not writing down everything you see and hear, you run the risk of missing something. But, remember, the purpose of lectures is to *explain*, not to fill you full of facts and figures. Most facts and figures can be looked up later. You should use lecture time to improve your *understanding* of a subject.

If a tutor says something like 'You don't have to write this down; it's in the handouts', believe them and don't write anything down – just listen.

If a tutor hasn't given you any handouts for a lecture, ask if you can have some. Tell them that you find the subject interesting but complex (flatter them). You never know, you might get lucky!

If your HE institution offers lecture notes for sale, buy them if you can. Pound for pound they are better value than both textbooks and beer. A tutor's lecture notes are likely to contain most of what you will need for the assessments.

Use knowledge trees, mind maps, verbal cues or anything else that lets you spend as much time as possible just listening.

Reflecting

A good way of organizing knowledge is to reflect on it – that is, to cast your mind back over recent learning experiences and try to replay them to yourself. This has two effects. First, it gives you a better chance of remembering things. Second, it will help you connect what you have learned to other pieces of knowledge.

You can reflect when you are doing something else. For example, it's possible to reflect during physical activity. You can also reflect during 'dead' time like waiting in a queue.

HOW TO APPLY

When you were at school you might have developed the ability to learn new skills and knowledge quite quickly, but you might not have learned to apply them very well. This is a shame since, as we said earlier, tutors are very keen on testing this and employers value it above all else. As a student, therefore, you need to learn how to do it.

There are numerous reasons why application causes problems for students. You might recognize some of these in yourself.

Lack of experience

You may simply lack the experience necessary to understand where and how a particular piece of knowledge or skill can be applied.

Always ask tutors to explain the real world application of what they are teaching you.

Lack of understanding

If you don't *understand* something you won't have related it to everything else you know. In other words you won't have *organized* it in your mind. In the previous section we explained that some things you have to understand and some things you don't. Some students take this too far and go into open book exams thinking that they don't need to understand anything at all. They assume that they can simply look up the required information and apply it to the questions in the exam but, unless there is an exact example in the textbook or notes, this won't work. You must learn to apply your skills and knowledge wherever they are applicable, not just in the tutor's examples.

Time pressures

You might not appreciate just how long it takes to really learn how to apply skills and knowledge as opposed to simply working through examples in a lecture or book.

If you aren't experienced at learning how to apply skills and knowledge take the time you would normally allow and treble it!

There is only one way to learn how to apply knowledge and that is to practise. In the long run this won't just help you to get better grades, it will also help you find and keep a good job.

Try to associate an example of everything you learn with one of its applications, perhaps by using a knowledge tree, mind map or verbal cue.

Don't try to understand complex proofs, theories and derivations unless you know you will need them for the assessments – just learn how to apply them.

PROBLEM SOLVING

Assignments and exam questions are designed to present you with a problem. In fact, many people would say the very purpose of HE is to teach you how to solve problems. In order to solve problems you will need to be good at *judging, applying* and *synthesizing* what you have learned. Of course, your ability to do this well is dependent on how well you dealt with lower levels of learning *(skills, knowledge, analysis* and *understanding)*.

You can fit problem solving into three broad categories: 'how to?', 'when to?' and 'what to?'. 'How to?' relates to mastering specific skills, such as reading, writing and long division. 'When to?' means knowing when and where to apply particular skills. Most jobs, from bank robbery to brain surgery, are based on 'how to?' and 'when to?' problem solving. But 'what to?' problems are the tough ones, and you are sure to get some of these on your course. Final-year projects, for instance, tend to pose a number of 'what to?' problems – the first one usually being what topic to choose. In order to solve a 'what to?' problem you should ask yourself a series of questions relating to the following aspects of the problem:

- context
- content
- self
- others

We can show how this works by using a 'what to?' problem from real life:

You are a student who always seems to have a problem handing certain assignments in on time. You want to improve this situation but are unsure what to do about it.

Context

- Where does this problem arise?
- How does this problem arise?
- When does this problem arise?
- Is it related to other problems?
- Is it a 'one off' or does it keep coming back?
- Have you seen it before?

The problem seems to happen mainly with business courses. You find it easy to do the initial work for the assignments but have difficulty in meeting the deadlines. The problem keeps arising in these cases.

Content

- What is the problem?
- Can you describe it in words?
- Can you quantify it?
- Can you describe it in terms of timing or time scales?

The problem appears to be related to the submission of business assignments using a word processor. You lack confidence in your ability to produce good and neat assignments. Because of this you tend to leave the production of the assignment until the last minute.

Self

- How does the problem make you feel?

- What difficulties does the problem cause you?

- Is it a real problem or do you just think it's a problem?

The problem puts you under stress. Difficulties are caused by missing deadlines for assignments. This is a real and pressing problem, since it affects both your academic and personal life.

Others

- Are other people experiencing the problem?

- Are other people causing the problem?

- Can other people solve the problem?

One or two of your friends also have trouble with word processors. While this is clearly your own problem it may be possible to get another student to help you gain confidence with the technology. Also, might you consider:

- approaching the University computer centre?

- buying a cheap self-help book?

- joining a computer club?

- enrolling on a basic word processing course?

Answering these questions pinpoints the problem and helps you identify both the conditions and the necessary 'what to?' for a solution.

You can now see clearly that your failure to hand in assignments on time stems from your poor word processing skills. What to do about the problem also becomes clear; you must learn to use the wordprocessor and gain confidence. Also, you can begin to identify possible sources of help.

Figure 3.3 shows a mind map that might help you to solve problems.

Figure 3.3   Problem solving mind map

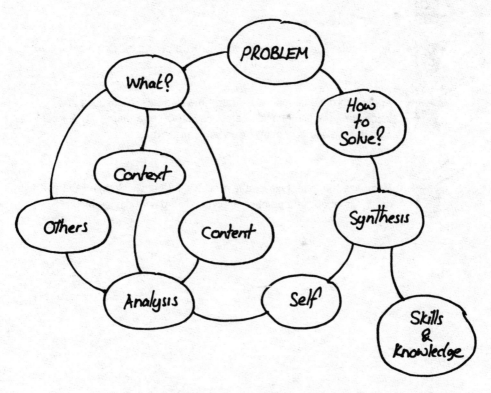

As with most things, the best way of learning how to solve a problem is by practising. Most people know that practice makes perfect but think that it only applies to physical tasks. In fact, working out with your mind, as well as your body, will help you gain the mental agility you need to solve problems well.

Memorize a shopping list, perhaps by using verbal cues, rather than writing it down.

Play word games in your head. For instance, using the letters of a long word, try to make as many small words as you can.

Play Scrabble or other word games.

Add numbers in your head occasionally rather than using a calculator.

Apply a formula in your head from time to time. For instance, try calculating the compound interest on £1000 at a rate of 10 per cent per annum, and see how many years you can do it for.

Memorize the four-stage problem analysis (Context, Content, Self, Others) described above and practise applying it in day-to-day problems.

MANAGING TIME

Time is the most precious commodity in your life. If you waste it you are squandering something very important and valuable. It's amazing how much time some students waste, which is a shame because your student years are the ideal time to develop good time management habits. To manage time successfully you must learn four principles:

- planning
- prioritization
- optimization
- time budgeting

Planning

Planning comes first because good time management depends on knowing what you need to do in advance. You will accomplish much more if you have a plan.

We all plan in different ways. Some people plan their time down to the last minute. For these people a comprehensive diary or personal organizer is a useful tool. Others prefer a more broad-brush approach whereby they only plan significant tasks. Whichever approach suits you best a regular routine will help by eliminating time spent planning everyday tasks and activities. Establish a routine that includes times for study, socializing, playing sport, shopping, reflecting and so on. Don't try to stick to your routine come what may; consider it as a framework that reduces the need to constantly make trivial decisions. Making these trivial decisions takes up the mental energy you should be saving for the more important things in life.

The importance of routine cannot be over-emphasized. When you were at school most of your time was regulated by routines imposed by other people. You need to take advantage of your new-found freedom to develop your own routines in order to succeed both as a student and graduate of HE. Many poor performances and failures are due to bad time management.

Prioritizing

Not everything you do is equally important. Handing in a critical assignment on time might be more important than playing a game of squash. But both pale into insignificance beside the need to visit a family member or close friend who is suddenly taken ill. We must all make prioritizing decisions about what to do with our time. How good are you at doing this?

If you have trouble deciding the relative priority of tasks, ask your tutors, friends or anyone else who might be able to help.

Ask yourself this question: 'What will happen to me if I don't do this on time?'. Here are some possible answers:

1. damage to my physical well being

2. damage to my self esteem

3. damage to my personal life

4. damage to my career

5. damage to my academic career

6. damage to my family's opinion of me

7. damage to my friends' opinion of me

8. damage to my tutor's opinion of me

Once you have identified the possible consequences, ask yourself 'Does it really matter to me that much?'.

As you go down this list, the implications of not doing something on time become less and less harmful to you. The precise order varies from person to person. Use your own list to prioritize your tasks.

If you think that everything you have to do is equally important, think again – you are probably wrong. But if this genuinely is the case, pick the first task you come to, concentrate on it exclusively and stop worrying about the others. If you do have too much to do you will need to find some more time. This means negotiating with whoever set the particular tasks. If it was you who set the tasks in the first place your negotiations should be fairly straightforward!

Don't underestimate the amount of time it takes to do things, particularly if you haven't done them before. Many businesses have failed because they didn't allow sufficent time to complete their contracts. Always try to allow a bit extra and never try to squeeze work into less time than you know you will need; this will inevitably lead to low grades and high stress.

Peer pressure might be a problem for you; being assertive and making sure you meet your priorities can be difficult. But remember that your real friends will be sensitive to your needs and respect you for being consistent and responsible. Working to other people's priorities is a very bad idea and often causes stress-related illnesses later in life – so don't start doing it now.

Optimizing

Optimizing your time depends partly on knowing your strengths and partly on developing good habits. If you are more alert and creative in the mornings, schedule work requiring these qualities for this time of day.

The Duke of Wellington was probably the most successful British soldier ever. He was also an excellent time manager. When Lord Stanhope asked him how he had achieved so much in his life, he made the famous response; 'My rule always was to do the business of the day in the day.' The message is; don't put it off – do it sooner rather than later.

You should also try to make use of what would otherwise be dead time.

If you are going to the doctors take a textbook to read in the waiting room.

Some tasks are just a pain in the neck. We don't all like writing letters, filling in forms and paying bills.

Set aside a specific time to do unpleasant jobs – preferably a time when you are unlikely to be distracted and therefore tempted not to finish. Setting aside time for these chores also means that you won't waste time worrying about when to do them.

Time budgeting

Not only do you need to fit your study into the other aspects of your life, you also need to pace yourself. This means planning for study and allowing sufficient breaks for exercise and social activities to refresh both your body and mind. The importance of balancing study with other activities cannot be overstated. The maxim 'All work and no play makes Jack a dull boy' is fairly well known. The maxim 'All work and no play means Jack might not get an A is not so well known but is equally true!

Budgeting the use of your time is like a form of cost–benefit analysis. Not every task you undertake is equally beneficial. This is something that many people fail to learn. Be aware of the relative benefits of everything you do and prioritize accordingly. Remember that you are not on this earth to fulfil other people's desires but to pursue your own. This is not the same as being selfish; you are perfectly entitled to choose your own goals and work towards them. To achieve your goals you need to budget your time and effort to ensure the maximum pay-off; this way, you have the chance of a happy life. Many people reach middle age and wish that they'd used their time better. It's never too late to start budgeting your time but it's much better to learn this while you are young.

Prioritize your goals in life. This will make prioritizing your time much easier because you will usually find that competing tasks relate to different goals.

Attending the first XV rugby practice relates to my goal of playing for the university or college team. But attending an important Student Union meeting relates to my desire to become a politician or a union leader. Which I choose will depend upon my judgement of the relative importance of these goals.

TIME SCHEDULING

Our bodies operate in cycles called biorhythms. In other words, our state of mental and physical alertness varies with time. The primary cycles are about 24 hours long but there are longer and shorter cycles woven into these. Biorhythms affect our performance greatly and can also simply make us feel elated or depressed. Our ability to carry out even routine tasks can therefore vary significantly depending on precisely when we do them. Some people study better in the mornings and some late at night. Some people study best in short bursts, others do better with the 'long slog'.

Try studying at different times of the day. Notice how easily you are able to concentrate and how you feel at the end. If you feel tired and dissatisfied and were easily distracted, try a different time.

4 ASSESSMENT METHODS

The way tutors mark work depends on the type of assessment method they are using at the time. Different tutors favour different assessment methods. To get the best grades possible you should identify exactly which method is being used, and then gear your work to it.

By assessment methods we don't mean an exam, a presentation or a written assignment. We are referring to what the tutor is trying to evaluate about your performance and what you need to do to get the best possible grade. If the subject is mathematics, and you are asked for a rigorous proof of a theorem, it may be obvious how to get top marks. However, in many subjects the tutor's requirements may not be so clear.

LEARNING OUTCOMES

There are many different assessment methods used in HE, which we will cover in more detail later, but one common factor is the concept of outcomes – what you should be able to do at the end of a particular part of your course. You will do better if you see assessments in these terms. Ask yourself constantly 'What should I be able to do at the end of this assignment, lecture, tutorial or course?'.

The problem is that tutors often don't tell you what the learning outcomes are – sometimes they don't even know themselves! This situation often leads students to ask such questions as; 'What exactly do you want us to do in this assignment?'. If you don't know what the learning outcomes are, your grade can end up being merely a matter of luck!

If you haven't been told, ask the tutor what the learning outcomes are. If they can't answer this, politely ask them to give you an answer sometime in the near future.

CRITERIA

Criteria are what tutors should use to mark your assignments and exam questions against the learning outcomes.

The following, typical, marking scheme sets out the criteria a tutor might use to mark a business strategy assignment based on a case study:

- *analysis of case*
- *selection of appropriate strategy*
- *description of strategy*
- *implementation plan*
- *presentation of report*

Obviously, to get good grades you should find out what the marking criteria are before you start any work. But this might not be so simple for the following reasons:

- The tutor may not understand the concept of criteria!
- The tutor may understand criteria but have difficulty writing them down.
- The tutor has written down the criteria, but you have no idea what he or she is talking about.
- The tutor may disagree with the idea of defining criteria as this reduces what some of them call 'academic freedom'.
- The tutor may genuinely be leaving the question very 'open' in order to test your ability to structure your own response and justify your approach.

If you don't know or understand what the criteria are, ask your tutor for assistance. Unless they are genuinely testing your ability to structure your response and justify your approach, they will probably help.

Ask the tutor a question like 'How would you go about answering this assignment?'. It may not work, but some tutors will see it as a challenge to describe an approach without giving too much away. You are flattering the tutor by asking them to display their expertise.

When you are given criteria you will usually be given weightings for them as well.

- *analysis of case*   *20%*
- *selection of appropriate strategy*   *30%*
- *description of strategy*   *15%*
- *implementation plan*   *20%*
- *presentation of report*   *15%*

If you are given weightings, use them to determine how much time and effort to put into each aspect of your assignment or exam question.

If you know the weightings, ask yourself these two questions:

1. *'Does this criterion have a high weighting value?'*
   If a criterion, such as 'presentation', only carries 5 per cent of the marks don't bother too much about what your assignment looks like, but if it carries 30 per cent make sure it's well presented.

2. *'Does this criterion play to my strengths – am I good at it?'*
   If you are weak on implementation plans, and this criterion only carries an average weighting, focus on the others first.

In the absence of any criteria or weightings pay particular attention to presentation and structure. You will see why later.

RANGE INDICATORS

As we have seen, knowing the assessment criteria will help you to match your work to the tutor's expectations and, to get the best grade possible, you must make sure that your response addresses each criterion. However, to understand exactly what the tutor wants, you need to know about 'range indicators'.

Your grade will depend on the tutor's judgement as to how well you have addressed each criterion and he or she may give you range indicators to help you do this. Range indicators tell you how many marks you will be awarded for a particular level of achievement against each criterion.

Suppose you are delivering an oral presentation. There might be a marking criterion called use of OHP (OverHead Projector). Here's a set of range indicators which might tell you what is required to achieve second-class marks for this criterion:

1. *Show all the slides in focus.*

2. *Place the slides on the OHP so that all their contents are projected on the screen.*

3. *Use text that is large enough to be read from the back of the room.*

4. *Discuss the slides without obscuring the audience's view of the screen.*

Here's the additional set of range indicators which might tell you how to achieve first-class marks:

1. *Use professional standard slides prepared on a computer.*

2. *Use colour.*

3. *Make extensive use of pictures and diagrams.*

In reality there may be a comprehensive set of range indicators which describe performances ranging from a bare pass to a perfect answer. Tutors use criteria weightings and range indicators to make marking easier and more consistent – which itself is good news. However, you can use them to even better effect as a basis for your answers. You can even use range indicators to mark your own work! Ask yourself questions like 'Have I done what's required to get the best marks?'.

If the tutor doesn't provide range indicators, ask for them.

If you don't get range indicators ask your tutor to show you an assignment which was awarded first-class marks. This gives you something to aim at and means you are more likely to get a higher grade. Listen carefully to what the tutor says about the assignment!

If your tutor won't show you an assignment like this, try to find a student who got first-class marks the year before.

COMPETENCE-BASED ASSESSMENT

In competence-based assessment the criteria are defined and marked in a binary fashion. The idea here is that you can either do something or you can't.

The following is a competence-based marking scheme for a word processing assignment:

- *Can input and edit text*   *Yes/No*
- *Can use document templates*   *Yes/No*
- *Can use graphics*   *Yes/No*
- *Can use tables*   *Yes/No*
- *Can do mail merges*   *Yes/No*

You can see that, for each criterion such as 'Can input and edit text', the tutor decides whether or not you can do it. There is no concept of grades here. You won't be assessed on how well you can use graphics for example. If you meet all the criteria you pass. If you don't, you usually fail the whole assessment. This type of assessment was first used in training, rather than education, but now it's popular in HE as well.

You will probably be given the criteria before the assessment. All you have to do is learn what the marking scheme tells you to, and you will undoubtedly pass!

5 UNDERSTANDING QUESTIONS

Because nearly all the questions you will be asked in HE will be open, you should understand what open questions are. First, we will see how they differ from the 'closed' questions you might be more used to.

CLOSED QUESTIONS

Many of the questions you were at asked school were closed – in other words, they had right and wrong answers. These types of question are designed to test your *knowledge* and *skills* and may be answered by:

- looking up
- memorizing
- calculating
- deriving

OPEN QUESTIONS

Open questions are designed to test higher levels of learning and have a number of characteristics:

- You can interpret them in different ways.
- You can answer them in different ways.
- They encourage you to research and discuss subjects.
- There are often no right or wrong answers – only views of the issues concerned.

As you can see, the first problem you have in tackling an open question is understanding what the question is in the first place. The rest of this chapter will help you to interpret open questions correctly. Unless you understand the question you are being asked, your chances of producing a good answer are fairly low. Answering the wrong question is a common cause of bad grades in HE. You must always find out what the right question is before you even think about answering it.

But what is the right question? As far as you are concerned the right question is the one that's in the tutor's head. There are two reasons why you might have trouble finding out what this is. First, the tutor might have phrased the question badly. Second, the tutor might be testing your ability to analyse questions; in other words, part of the question is; 'Do you understand this question?'.

Sometimes tutors do ask stupid questions but it's extremely rare and, when it happens, they don't admit it! If you are feeling brave or are really stuck you can always try asking the tutor for a plain English explanation of a question, but questions such as 'What do you want us to do?' will probably just annoy them. Correctly interpreting questions will usually be your responsibility and is dealt with in the following sections.

TERMINOLOGY

Tutors in HE often use long complex words with which you may not be familiar. Don't let this worry you; simply find out what the word means.

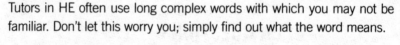

Look the words up in a dictionary.

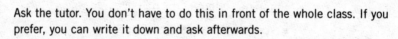

Ask the tutor. You don't have to do this in front of the whole class. If you prefer, you can write it down and ask afterwards.

Asking a tutor about the meaning of words is not the same as asking them to explain the question, and this has two advantages over the previous trick. First, the tutor's definition of a word might be different from the dictionary's. Second, some tutors will be flattered by your question and you will rise in their esteem.

COMMON TYPES OF QUESTION

Even if you understand what the words mean, you still might not understand the question. We can't cover every question you might come across in this book, but we can look at the common types of question and explain what they mean in plain English.

Compare and contrast

These questions are basically testing your *knowledge*. Consider the question:

Compare and contrast the Labour Party's and Conservative Party's approaches to achieving full employment.

This question is really saying:

1. Tell me what the Labour Party would do to achieve full employment and why they think it will work.

2. Tell me what the Conservative Party would do to achieve full employment and why they think it will work.

Notice that there are a number of *dimensions* to this question:

- How many different views are required? (In this example it's two – the Labour Party's and the Conservative Party's.)

- How do the views differ and how are the views similar?

- Why do they think their views are right?

As you can see, you need to identify all the dimensions in a question before you can answer it fully.

Discuss

These questions are the next step on from compare and contrast but are still essentially testing your *knowledge*. The key difference is in the first dimension. Unlike 'compare and contrast' questions, it is you, and not the tutor, who has to identify the source of the different opinions. You are not explicitly told that a number of different views exist at all.

The funding of the NHS (National Health Service) has been cited as a prime example of wasting taxpayers' money. However, many politicians believe that the NHS, as well as providing a valuable social service, is an essential mechanism for supporting the UK economy. *Discuss.*

This question is really saying:

1. Identify a number of people who believe that the NHS should be funded by taxation.

2. Identify a number of people who believe that the NHS should not be funded by taxation.

3. For each person you have chosen, say why they believe it's good or bad for the UK economy.

Unless you are told otherwise, try to find two or three opinions 'for' and two or three 'against'.

Critically appraise or evaluate

Questions including the terms like 'critically appraise' or 'evaluate' are designed to test *understanding* and *judgement*. These questions are asking what views of an issue you have and why you hold them.

Critically appraise the statement 'The funding of the NHS is a prime example of wasting taxpayers' money'.

This question is really saying:

1. Find a number of people who believe the NHS should be funded by taxation.

2. Find a number of people who believe the NHS should not be funded by taxation.

3. For each person you have chosen, state why they believe it's good or bad for the UK economy.

4. Say who you agree with and produce some evidence to support your opinion. (Evidence will be covered in Chapter 6.)

Using an example

These questions test your ability to apply what you have learned. Note the word 'an' in the term 'using an example'. This means take **one** example. This type of question asks you to discuss a particular issue and use a real example to highlight the points you are making.

'Professional sales executives are worth their weight in gold and no modern business can do without them.' Discuss this statement with reference to an organization with which you are familiar.

This question is really saying:

1. Find a business that uses sales executives (if necessary, by doing some research).

2. Say what benefits and disadvantages the sales executives have brought to that business. Use a real example of each benefit and disadvantage.

3. Say whether you think sales executives are worth their weight in gold and justify your opinion by producing some further examples taken from the business you have chosen.

Using examples

These are the ultimate application questions. They ask you to discuss the issue under consideration using a number of diverse examples to highlight the points you are making.

Using examples, discuss the statement 'IT (Information Technology) does more harm than good'.

This question is really saying:

1. Find a number of diverse businesses that use IT.

2. Say what benefits and disadvantages IT has brought to each business, using real examples.

3. Try to find examples where one aspect of IT has been beneficial to one business but not to another.

4. Say whether you think IT does more harm than good, and justify your opinion by using further examples.

Define, design, formulate, produce

Questions that begin with words such as 'define', 'design', 'formulate', or 'produce' are asking you to create something – they are testing your ability to *synthesize*. These questions can be very tough because, in a sense, there is no right question. The tutor will be testing your ability to define and constrain the question yourself. In other words, it's up to you what you do and how you approach it. Remember that your ability to reach a reasonable definition of the question is being assessed.

For these problems there is no existing solution. You must create the solution yourself by combining relevant knowledge and experience in a new way. In short, you are being asked to throw all of your previous learning into a melting pot in order to devise an original solution to a new problem. Needless to say, these questions are the most challenging. To get good grades here you will need to do a great deal of research and apply all of your problem solving skills.

Find out how similar problems have been solved in the past. It's often possible to take the solution to a similar problem and then modify it in order to solve the problem you are faced with.

Using the attached case study (Clever Co. PLC) define an appropriate marketing strategy to support their export drive.

This question is really saying:

1. Read the case study and say what the key characteristics of Clever Co. PLC's business are.

2. Find some real businesses that have some similar characteristics to Clever Co. PLC.

3. For the real businesses you have identified, say what their export marketing strategies are.

4. Design a new export marketing strategy for Clever Co. PLC by combining characteristics of the real businesses' export marketing strategies.

5. Say why you think the marketing strategy you have defined will work, using examples from the real businesses and any other evidence you can find.

BREAKING DOWN QUESTIONS

In the previous section we considered common types of questions, and the examples we used fitted neatly into one of the categories we defined. However, as you might have guessed, many of the questions you will face may be a complex mixture of the question types we have discussed. We will now show you an analysis technique to help you break down and understand questions. Of course, we can only teach you the principles. It's up to you to apply them to the different questions you will come across. Consider this question:

Critically appraise, in a brief report, a biographical or autobiographical book of a marketing role model.

You might look at this question and think 'How can this be a jumbled up question? Surely it's a 'critically appraise' question. In fact it is not. Despite its shortness, this is a very complex and subtle question which most students would be unable to interpret without some help. Many students would respond to a question like this by writing some sort of book review, stating what they liked about the book and what they didn't. They might even go on to say whether or not they enjoyed reading it. But this is **not** what the question is asking you to do. The tutor won't care if you enjoyed reading it or not; they won't even care if you have sacrificially burned it. Use the following technique to analyse this question to find out what it's really asking.

1. Pick out all the verbs. In this case, the verb is 'appraise'.

A highlighting pen is useful for this.

2. Now highlight any adverbs. In this case, the adverb is 'critically'.

   Now you know that you are being asked to critically appraise something. At this stage it's worth reconsidering what the term 'critically appraise' means; discuss the issue under consideration then describe your views on it and why you hold them.

3. Now highlight any instructions as to what format your response should take. In this case, the word is 'report'. (Report writing is covered in Chapter 7.)

4. Now highlight any other instructions regarding the format of your response. The word in this case is 'brief'. But what does 'brief' mean? Ask the tutor to give you a word count limit, but brief usually means about 1200 words.

   So far, you know that you have to critically appraise something in a 1200 word report.

5. Now highlight the parts of the question that tell you what you have to critically appraise. In this case there are three aspects to consider:

   ■ It has to be a biography or autobiography.

   ■ The word 'marketing' has been mentioned – but what is marketing? We will look at this in just a moment.

   ■ The book has to be about a role model (someone famous and well respected for something – in this case, marketing).

Your task has now emerged. You have to find a biographical or autobiographical book about a role model famous for marketing and then critically appraise the book in a 1200 word report. But you are still missing something. Remember, 'critically appraise' means discuss the issue under consideration then describe your views on it and why you hold them. You might now be thinking, 'But what exactly is the issue under consideration?'. The issue is marketing. This is the last piece in the jigsaw. This question is very clever. In a nut-shell it's saying, 'What do you think marketing is?', but it's also asking you to perform some much more specific tasks, namely:

- *Choose a marketing role model by picking an appropriate book.* Your judgement is being tested here. The act of choosing an appropriate book to critically appraise is part of the question's answer, because your choice will demonstrate which role models you think are particularly good or bad marketers.

- *Pick out a small number of examples which you think make the role model excellent at marketing.* This is a 'using examples' question.

- *Say how the role model's views differ from more common views.* This is a 'compare and contrast' question.

- *If appropriate, say why you think some or all of the role model's views fail to match your concept of excellent marketing.*

You can see how apparently simple questions can be quite complex and tricky to deal with. Don't be tempted to dive into questions before you are certain that you have fully analysed and understood them.

COMMON MISTAKES

Finally, in answering the right question, remember not to make common mistakes. A surprising number of students have bad habits that lose them marks. Let's take a look at some of these now.

Writing out the question

Don't write out assignment or exam questions in your answer. The tutor knows what the question is because they wrote it! As well as being unnecessary this has a number of other drawbacks:

- It's a waste of your time.
- The tutor might include it in any word count limit.
- The tutor will probably think you are a wally.

Explaining terminology

This is a similar mistake to writing out the question. Unless you have strong evidence to the contrary, don't explain the terminology used in the question. The tutor will assume that you know what the terms mean and it is 100 per cent certain that he or she does too!

Do you think that Porter's value chain can be applied to the case study (Clever Co. PLC)?

Some students would start their response to this question with an explanation of Porter's value chain. This is a waste of time because it is not what the question is asking. You are being asked to **apply** Porter's value chain, not define it.

Not following instructions

Tutors will very often give you specific instructions with assignments and exam questions that relate to the format of your response such as:

- word count limits
- whether or not your response should be typed
- where you should hand your assignment in
- who your assignment should be addressed to

Carefully follow all of these instructions. If you don't, you may land yourself a whole raft of problems. One of the better outcomes is that your tutor merely becomes slightly irritated and knocks a mark off. Some of the harsher tutors may have a marking criterion called 'followed all the instructions' and knock more than one mark off! At the other end of the scale is the possibility that your work will be 'lost in the system' – which is, remember, very large and bureaucratic! If this happens your work will probably be failed with a 'zero' grade. Although you are likely to get a grade in the end, if you produce a copy of your work along with evidence that you handed it in on time, this will involve a considerable amount of time, effort, embarrassment and stress.

6 ANSWERING QUESTIONS

In Chapter 5 we showed you some tricks for finding the right question. We couldn't analyse all the questions you might face, and obviously we can't answer them all either. We make no apologies for this. There is no point in learning how to answer specific questions – you must learn how to answer **all** of them. Remember that there are often no right or wrong answers to open questions. We might answer an open question by putting forward totally opposite views to you, yet both of us might get first-class marks! In general, tutors will want to see that:

- you have done sufficient research
- the research you have done is appropriate to the question
- the research is balanced and not biased towards one particular view
- you have interpreted and understood the research material correctly
- you have reached reasonable conclusions
- the points you are making are supported by evidence

We mentioned evidence earlier. Now's a good time to find out exactly what it is.

EVIDENCE

Just like solicitors and barristers in law courts, you need evidence to back up the points you are making. To explain the importance of evidence we will use one of the example questions from Chapter 5:

'Professional sales executives are worth their weight in gold and no modern business can do without them.' Discuss this question with reference to an organization with which you are familiar.

If you want to get a low grade, state in your response: 'Sales executives are worth their weight in gold because, without them, most businesses would go bankrupt.' This is an unsupported statement (an assertion). It doesn't matter whether or not it's true – it is not backed up by any evidence. Always back up your arguments with evidence. Evidence comes in three basic forms:

- statistical information
- examples
- the views of eminent people in the field under discussion

We will now show you how you can use these types of evidence to answer our example question. (By the way, the evidence in our answers is not really true.)

Statistical information

Use statistics to support your answers.

Sales executives **are** worth their weight in gold. Sales staff make up 10 per cent of the workforce in the world's top 500 companies, but the figure is only 5 per cent for the average business.

Examples

Use an example to show that your answer is backed up by fact.

Sales executives **are** worth their weight in gold. 10 per cent of the staff at the market-leading Clever Co. PLC are in sales, but the figure is only 5 per cent for their major competitors.

Eminent persons

Use quotations from people who are respected in the field.

Sales executives **are** worth their weight in gold. The Chairman and Chief Executive of the market-leading Clever Co. PLC, Sir John Bold, is on record as saying, 'Sales staff are the key to a successful business'.

PRESENTING EVIDENCE

You now know that you have to back up your comments and arguments with evidence. But how does the tutor know that your evidence is real and that you haven't merely invented it? Just like lawyers and barristers you need to state the source of your evidence – in other words you must show where it's come from. There are certain conventions for doing this in HE, and following them will almost certainly gain you extra marks. Here are a number of examples.

Direct source references

This is the simplest type of referencing; after your evidence, write:

- the word 'source' followed by a colon
- the source itself (in this case the mythical *Journal of Clever Companies*)
- the date when the information was produced (not the date you found the information out)

Sales executives **are** worth their weight in gold. 10 per cent of the staff at the market-leading Clever Co. PLC are in sales, but the figure is only 5 per cent for their major competitors.

Source: *Journal of Clever Companies*, 1994.

Quotations

Here's the correct way of using quotations.

1. Place the quotation itself (which must be word-perfect) inside quotation marks. This may sound obvious, but some students forget.

2. Write the name of the person who made the statement.

3. Write the person's title or position.

4. Write the name of the organization to which they belong.

'Sales executives are the key to a successful business.'
Sir John Bold, Chairman and Chief Executive, Clever Co. PLC.

Bibliographies

You might already include bibliographies in your work, but you will probably score a few more points with the tutor by presenting your bibliography in a standard format. This won't take much longer than doing it any other way. The following example is just one format but there are many others:

SMART, B. (1994) <u>Good Book on Business.</u> Big Publishers.
ISBN 1-2345-6789-1.

In this example the capital letters, commas, full stops, brackets and underlining all have to be done correctly in order to conform to this standard, so be sure to get it right.

Citing

Citing is a fairly technical and complex means of referencing sources in written material. It's essential when writing research papers or postgraduate dissertations, and is often worth a few extra marks at undergraduate level.

As for bibliographies there are many conventions for citing but, unless you have been told otherwise, this one will work fine – after you have presented some evidence:

1. Write the 'reference number' of your source in superscript immediately after the evidence.

2. Write the title of the text and the page number where your evidence appears in the page footer.

3. Place the text you have referenced in a bibliography alongside its appropriate reference number.

Figure 6.1   A citation

Sales executives *are* worth their weight in gold. Ten per cent of the staff at the market leading Clever Co PLC are in sales, but the figure is only five per cent for their major competitors [2]

---

[2]: *Journal of Clever Companies*, pp. 121 – 122.   Page 5 of 9

BIBLIOGRAPHY

1. SMART, B. (1994) Good Book on Business. Big Publishers. ISBN 1-2345-6789-1.

2. Journal of Clever Companies (1994), Industrial Press, ISBN 2-3456-7891-2.

3. CLEVER, A. (1995) Great Book on Marketing. Small Publishers. ISBN 3-4567-8912-1.

If you want to learn some of these citing conventions, ask a librarian. They generally know more about this than tutors.

PLAGIARISM AND COLLUSION

You might not have heard of plagiarism at school, but, in HE, it's very important that you understand the issues surrounding this rather vague area.

What is plagiarism?

Plagiarism is difficult to define, but basically it's stealing someone else's ideas – in other words, representing someone else's work as your own. You can think of it as intellectual theft or fraud. Here are some of the common ways in which you might plagiarize. As you can see, these range from the blatantly obvious to the fairly subtle:

- Copy another student's work and put your name on it.
- Copy another student's work, change it around a bit (perhaps using a thesaurus or dictionary) and put your name on it.
- Include some text out of a book in your work, but don't say where it has come from – that is, fail to reference the source.
- Take some text out of a book, change it around a bit and include it in your own work.

You can plagiarize from all sources of information:

- books
- magazines
- newspapers
- journals
- videos
- material on computer disks
- TV programmes

What is collusion?

Collusion differs from plagiarism but is often treated in a similar way by HE institutions. Here's an example of how you could be guilty of collusion:

You are set an **individual** assignment by a tutor that consists of two questions. You answer the first question and get your friend to answer the second question. When you have both finished you combine the two answers to form one assignment. You photocopy it and both hand a copy in as your own work.

If you want to be a bit more clever, you might alter one of the copies slightly to make them look different. Of course, if you are using a word processor this is much easier; you can use the electronic thesaurus and grammar checkers to help you. (By the way this is not a trick!)

As you can see, collusion is working with another person when you are meant to be doing something on your own.

Penalties

As you will no doubt have gathered, tutors consider plagiarism and collusion to be serious offences for two principal reasons. First, if you are found guilty of plagiarism or collusion many tutors will think of you as a thief and deceiver. Second, the purpose of plagiarism and collusion is to gain an unfair advantage over your fellow students.

In short, if you are caught plagiarizing or colluding you will probably become very unpopular with both tutors and students. But that's just the beginning of your problems. If you are suspected of plagiarism or collusion you will probably be investigated by a panel of senior academics who have the power to impose very severe penalties. These vary according to a number of factors:

- *The particular HE institution you are studying with:* in some institutions you can get away with quite a lot before they throw you out, but others take it much more seriously.
- *The particular tutors who deal with the plagiarism case:* like judges, some tutors are more lenient than others.
- *Your age:* if you are relatively young, you will probably be treated more leniently than a more mature student.
- *Your year of study:* the further through a course you are, the greater the likely penalty.
- *The course you are following:* the penalties are likely to be greater on postgraduate courses than on undergraduate courses.
- *Whether or not you have a 'previous record'.*
- *The precise nature of the plagiarism or collusion:* if you have plagiarized a small section of an assignment you will be in better shape than if you photocopied another student's work.

Here are a few example cases of plagiarism and collusion with likely penalties that you might expect:

Case 1

- You are young.
- You are a first-year undergraduate.
- You have plagiarized a small section of an assignment.

Penalty: your assignment is failed.

Case 2

- You are a final-year undergraduate.
- You are already unpopular with the tutors.
- You and a friend collude on a individual assignment to produce a piece of work which consists entirely of paraphrased material from a textbook.

Penalty: you are restricted to getting a non-honours degree.

Case 3:

- You are a mature student with several years' work experience.
- You are on a postgraduate course.
- You steal and photocopy another student's assignment and put your name on it.

Penalty: you are expelled.

Detection

Now you know the penalties, what are the chances of getting away with plagiarism and collusion? First, you should understand a very important principle. As is the case with all laws, rules and regulations, ignorance is no excuse for plagiarism and collusion. If you plagiarize or collude accidentally it will make little difference to the penalty you receive. It's your responsibility to understand what plagiarism and collusion are and take the necessary steps to avoid them.

Before we tell you how tutors identify plagiarism and collusion, we ought to consider why they bother with it at all. After all, dealing with it can involve tutors in much time and aggravation. However, don't imagine that they will overlook it. Most of them will penalize you for the following reasons. First, they get paid to do it. Part of a tutor's job includes the detection of plagiarism and collusion. Second, if an external examiner or colleague suspects that a tutor has turned a blind eye they can be taken to task over it and might even be reprimanded themselves. Third, tutors tend to be very principled people who often feel they have a continuous and absolute duty to seek out and destroy plagiarism.

So how do tutors detect plagiarism and collusion? First, they tend to mark many assignments at a time, making it easy to spot similar work handed in by another student, even if it's been deliberately disguised. Second, tutors tend to read and discuss a great deal of material in their subject area and it's generally very easy for them to identify plagiarized work simply by its content. Third, when people plagiarize or collude there are usually noticeable changes in style – a tell-tale sign of plagiarism or collusion.

Our advice is: never plagiarize or collude. The penalties far outweigh the benefits and you are a cheat if you do it! Get the grades using our 'trix' – they are all honest and legal.

7 REPORTS

As a student you will often have to present your answers in the form of a report. But reports aren't just a method of presentation. Report writing is a very useful and powerful technique in itself. Knowing how to write reports properly will be a big help in both understanding and answering questions. Before we explain how to write reports, let's take a look at exactly what reports are.

WHAT IS A REPORT?

First, let's explore some myths and facts about reports:

Myth: Reports are just another name that business people use for essays.

Fact: Reports are very different from essays.

Myth: It's a good idea to make reports as long and complex as possible. This will impress tutors and give the document an air of professionalism.

Fact: Reports should be as short and simple as possible. Waffley reports are very likely to lose you marks.

Myth: Reports are easy to produce by following a few simple rules. It's basically the content that matters.

Fact: Producing a proper report is a complex and difficult task which few people are taught and even fewer master. Excellent work is often lost in poorly written reports.

To explain the nature of reports we will now demonstrate how they differ from the essays which you might have been more used to writing at school.

Purpose

Essays and reports have different purposes. Essays are often written with what's known as 'aesthetic quality'. Good essay writers pay considerable attention to the artistic and pleasing impression of their writing. They make sure their essays have a flowing style and use lots of subtle and emotive words. On the other hand, good reports simply communicate information in the most efficient way possible. There is no place for clever prose or romantic irony in report writing. Reports are designed to be quick and easy to read, not make people happy.

Language style

Both reports and essays should be grammatically correct, but because they have different purposes their language style is different. Essays tend to have a descriptive and flowing style. Reports, on the other hand, use a more direct approach. Here's a comment you might find in an essay:

Clever Co. PLC is a giant amongst retailers. With a massive turnover in excess of £1000m it dwarfs its nearest competitor.

Here's the equivalent comment made in a report:

Clever Co. PLC is the largest UK retailer. Its turnover is £1400m. Its nearest competitor's turnover is £600m.

Numbers

In essays numbers are generally written using words, but reports use actual numbers.

Here's a sentence you might find in an essay:

Clever Co. PLC has four directors.

Here's the equivalent sentence for a report:

Clever Co. PLC has 4 directors.

Emphasis

In essays the author often uses complex sentence structures to emphasize points. In reports this is done by simply boldening, underlining or capitalizing the typeface. Here's a sentence you might find in an essay:

Although it might seem hard to believe, Clever Co. PLC doesn't give away discount under any circumstances whatsoever.

Here are some equivalent sentences for a report:

Clever Co. PLC **never** give discounts.

Clever Co. PLC <u>never</u> give discounts.

Clever Co. PLC NEVER give discounts.

Italics

Italics are usually used in essays to indicate foreign words but in reports they are used to indicate names, titles or instructions to the reader. For instance, here's a sentence you might find in an essay.

For a full description of Clever Co. PLC's *modus operandi* see Appendix 1.

Here's the equivalent sentence for a report:

For a full description of Clever Co. PLC's modus operandi *see Appendix 1.*

Structure

Reports have a more obvious and rigid structure than essays. Structure is discussed in more detail on pages 81–83.

Acronyms and abbreviations

In essays, names and titles are always written out in full, but in reports acronyms and abbreviations are used as much as possible in order to save time both in writing and reading them.

The first time you use an acronym or abbreviation you should put the full text immediately after it in brackets. Capitals should be used only where there is a capital in the acronym. Notice how the 'of' in the following example doesn't have a capital letter because there is no 'O' in 'DTI'.

Clever Co. PLC has an excellent relationship with the DTI (Department of Trade and Industry).

Common abbreviations are used without explanation in reports. For instance, you would write '£1400m' rather than '£1400 million'. But make sure that the tutor will interpret your acronyms or abbreviations in the way you intended. For instance, 'OHP' might mean 'OverHead Projector' to a business studies tutor but 'OverHead Powerline' to an electrical engineering tutor!

Bullets and lists

Unlike essays, lists in reports aren't included within sentences. Instead they are written as an introduction followed by a series of bullet points. Here's a sentence you might find in an essay:

Clever Co. PLC's sales force have succeeded because they are well trained, well paid, aggressive and hardworking.

Here's the equivalent for a report:

Clever Co. PLC's sales force succeed because they are:

■ well trained

■ well paid

■ aggressive

■ hardworking

Bullet points are short 'punchy' statements and should not generally be longer than a single sentence.

Lists are similar to bullet points but should be used in preference to bullets where:

■ there is a definite sequence to the items

■ there is a distinct order of priority to the items

Clever Co. PLC's sales force succeed because they are:

1. well trained

2. well paid

3. aggressive

4. hardworking

If the items form a sentence within themselves or are longer than a single sentence, use full stops, otherwise leave them out.

PRESENTATION

As with all your work, good presentation **will** earn you extra marks. You can make reports look good by the careful use of fonts, colours, graphs, tables, pictures, logos and so on. Equally important is the way in which the report is laid out as a whole. Designing a good report is not easy. It will take a fair amount of time and effort, and you certainly don't want to do it every time you write one. So take some time to produce an attractive report design and then use this as a template for all your reports. As well as saving time in the long run, it will give your reports a consistent image – tutors will be impressed.

Don't use a lot of different fonts – one is usually enough. The same goes for colour – only use two or three at the most. The simplest styles are usually the best.

Look at some professionally produced reports and magazine articles for presentation ideas, but don't copy them exactly, as this might get you into trouble with the authors or publishers.

So let's take a look at why good presentation is so important.

Marks for presentation

Tutors very often have a marking criterion specifically for presentation. Typically it has a weighting of between 5 and 25 per cent. Just think – you could get 25 per cent of the available marks just by presenting your work well and, as you will see, preparing well presented work doesn't have to be time consuming.

Hidden marks

In the last section we talked about weightings for the 'presentation' criterion. In reality, the weighting for the presentation is likely to be higher because many tutors are emotionally affected by how work is presented. A well presented piece of work will probably encourage them to be more generous with the marks for other criteria. This is an entirely subconscious reaction. Even if there is no specific criterion for presentation the message is the same. Well presented work will improve your grades.

STRUCTURE

As we have said before, reports should have an obvious and rigid structure. Most reports have a hierarchical structure (you could describe them with a knowledge tree) and are made up of sections and subsections at various 'levels'. There are numerous formal conventions for structuring reports but, unless you are a research student working in a specialized field, there will probably be no need to learn any of these. In most cases you can structure reports however you like. For instance, you might number the sections in long reports but not in shorter ones (see Figure 7.1).

Figure 7.1   Report structure

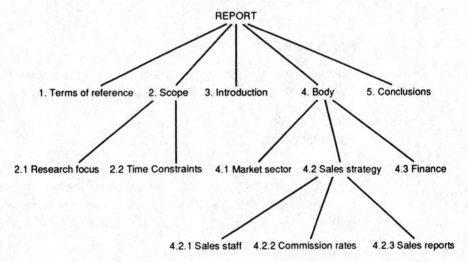

Developing a good structure should always be the first thing you do, for the reasons discussed below.

Saving time

A good report structure will tell you how much research you need to do and in what areas you need to do it. The extra time you spend on designing your report structure will almost always be recouped by time saved on irrelevant research.

Group work

If you are doing a group report it's essential to develop a good structure first. Without it you will duplicate effort and your report won't hang together very well. In other words, you will waste both time and marks.

Marks for structure

As with presentation, tutors very often have a marking criterion specifically for structure. This typically has a weighting of between 5 and 15 per cent, but up to 25 per cent is not uncommon. If your report has a good structure you will probably get most of these marks. Just think of it, you could get another 25 per cent of the available marks just for having a well thought-out structure!

Hidden marks

Again, the message here is the same as it is for presentation. The real marks for structure are likely to be higher than the tutor tells you.

Marks for content

Most tutors don't read every word of assignments. They speed-read them, looking for relevant points. Waffley reports are hard to read and even harder to mark; tutors generally become very bored and annoyed by them! If your reports are long and full of waffle the tutor will probably miss some of your relevant points.

Some students try to pad out their reports with waffle when they know they haven't done enough work. Far from fooling the tutor, this will probably be counterproductive. If the tutor sees a significant amount of waffle they often assume it's all like that, don't bother reading it too carefully and just give it a low grade. Of course, the student is not surprised by this because they know they didn't do enough work in the first place, but they could nevertheless have achieved a higher grade with a better structure. Remember, waffle is a waste of time and marks.

COMMON SECTIONS

We will now discuss some of the common sections you might put in a report. Reports vary greatly, so don't include sections just for the sake of it. For example, many students insist on including a 'Procedure' or 'Method' section, whether or not one is required, because this is what they were taught at school. 'Procedure' or 'Method' sections are necessary in some reports but irrelevant in others. Including such a section consisting merely of the words 'I produced the following report by going to the library, taking out some economics books, reading them, then writing this report' is both obvious and adds no value to the report. Furthermore, it won't impress the tutors. Remember, reports should be as short as possible.

Front page

Reports should always have a front page and here's what you need to put on them, unless you are told otherwise:

1. the marking tutor's name

2. your name

3. the title of your report

4. the date you produced it

Spell the tutor's name correctly. Spelling names wrongly is bad manners. It upsets some tutors so much that they will knock off a few marks for it!

Terms of reference

The terms of reference section is a statement of the contract you are making with the tutor. It says what you have done in your report and why you have done it. As you can see, this can be very useful when responding to open questions, but make sure it doesn't simply paraphrase the question.

This report has been written at the request of Mr John Smart-Tutor. It sets out to determine if Clever Co. PLC is likely to meet significant resistance when it attempts to introduce a new computer system into its marketing department.

Introduction

An introduction gives the tutor some useful background that helps set your report in context – that is, it makes the report easier to follow. For instance, a report on the 'Distribution Systems within Clever Co. PLC' might include a brief overview of the whole company. But, remember, an introduction should only include **relevant** information.

Clever Co. PLC is the largest retailer in the UK. Its turnover is £1400m. It has a very effective sales force which has been a key factor in helping it to successfully penetrate a number of European markets.

Scope

Scope is more complex. It refers to the extent and level of detail at which something is viewed. For instance, a microscope looks at small objects in great detail. Scope sections tell the tutor which topics your report covers and the amount of detail you will include on each of them. You can think of a report's scope as the contractual small print for the terms of reference.

Scope sections are very useful when you think that there might not be any one 'right' question. They not only help you constrain the question in the first place but, more importantly, they tell the tutor exactly how you have approached it. Telling the tutor what the question was can make the difference between a good and bad grade!

When considering the issue of 'Staff resistance to IT' at Clever Co. PLC I focused my research on the opinions of senior managers. A view from the unions would have been beneficial, but I could not cover this area within the timescales available.

In this example the tutor is being told explicitly that seeking a 'view from the unions' was considered but was not practical. Therefore the tutor can't knock off marks for ignorance of this research area. 'Scope' sections help eliminate instances of misunderstanding, where the tutor's idea of the question is different from your own. If you include one, most tutors will assess your performance against the scope you have defined – as long as it's reasonable, of course.

Method, procedure or approach

A 'Method', 'Procedure' or 'Approach' section can be essential in explaining how any research has been done.

Attitudes towards IT at Clever Co. PLC have been identified using **primary research** based on a comprehensive questionnaire *(see Appendix 1)*.

Assumptions

If your report relies on any assumptions that aren't obvious to the tutor you should always include an 'Assumptions' section.

Assumption: The reader is familiar with the principles of Net Present Value (NPV) in forecasting cash flows.

Body

The body of your report contains all your findings. Some students, still following school practices, actually call it the 'Findings' section, but it looks more professional if you give the sections of your report relevant titles. After all, it's obvious that a 'Findings' section contains findings!

Conclusions

A 'Conclusions' section contains your views of the issue under consideration along with some summarized evidence that supports them.

I believe that Clever Co. PLC would meet little or no resistance to introducing the proposed IT system provided that my recommendations are followed carefully. A virtually identical system was successfully implemented at Smart Co. PLC where similar recommendations were followed.

Recommendations

Some students insist on including a 'Recommendations' section come what may, but you should only include one if you have been explicitly asked to make some recommendations. If you do include one, it should always state what **benefits** would be achieved by following your recommendations; it shouldn't just be a series of assertions.

My recommendations are as follows:

- Fully brief all staff on the nature of the new IT system and why you need it.
- Get the views and ideas of **all** staff concerned.
- Include at least two members of operational staff on the project team.
- Consult the unions before making any changes to working practices.

Following these recommendations would both keep the staff happy and enable a faster implementation.

Summary

If your report is quite long you might want to include a summary, which is usually placed at the front. It should be no more than three-quarters of a side of A4 paper and should summarize only the key findings, conclusions and recommendations.

I believe that resistance to implementing an IT system at Clever Co. PLC can be eliminated by the involvement and consultation of all personnel.

Appendices

Appendices should contain relevant, but 'non-essential', evidence which supports some of the key points you are making.

Many students attach appendices to all their reports whether they are necessary or not, in the belief that it will make their report look more professional, and many more use them incorrectly. To decide whether or not something belongs in an appendix, ask yourself the following question: 'Will the tutor have to refer to it in order to continue reading, or can they refer to it later?' If the tutor has to flick to the back of the report in order to carry on reading, the information should not be in an appendix. There is nothing more frustrating for a tutor than reading a discussion of a particular diagram, graph or table in the middle of a report when the information itself is in an appendix at the end. If you do this you will probably lose some of the marks allocated for structure and are also quite likely to annoy the tutor. This is an example of the incorrect use of an appendix:

You will see from *diagram 1 (see Appendix 1)* how the Personnel Manager fits into the company hierarchy.

See the improvement in the following example in which an appendix has deliberately not been used:

Diagram 1 (above) shows how the Personnel Manager fits into the company hierarchy.

The following is an example of the correct use of an appendix:

Using a simple questionnaire, the Personnel Department have deduced that most staff favour flexible working practices (*see Appendix 1 for questionnaire*).

Notice how the reader can choose to look at the questionnaire in the appendix at this point, but doesn't have to in order to make sense of what is being said.

Table of contents

If your report is longer than about ten pages you might want to put in a table of contents.

Headers and footers

In Chapter 6 (page 61) we discussed how footers can be used for citing, but a more important use of headers and footers is for page numbering.

You must not only number the pages of your report but also put its total number of pages on **every** page. Do this in either the header or footer of the pages (see Figure 7.2).

Figure 7.2   Page numbering

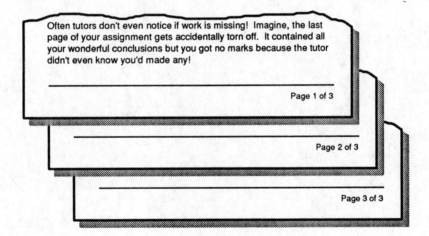

This procedure ensures that the tutor can be certain that all of your work is present. Tutors often collect and mark hundreds of assignments at a time. These assignments might have passed through several people's hands before reaching them. Combine this with the fact that HE institutions are notorious for losing things and the upshot is that the tutor could well end up with only part of your report to mark! Of course, this could be disastrous for you because tutors can only mark what's in front of them. Often, tutors don't even notice if work is missing. Suppose the last page of your assignment is accidentally torn off. It contained all your wonderful conclusions but you were awarded no marks for these because the tutor didn't even know you'd made any!

As well as adding page numbers, always keep copies of your work. Then, if the original gets lost, you can simply produce a copy.

WRITING A REPORT

Designing the structure of a report is a complex, difficult and often time-consuming task which you will probably initially find a little difficult. Don't give up. Like most things it becomes easier with practice. So, how do you go about writing a good report? First, you plan the basic structure, following these steps.

1. Make sure you fully understand the question the assignment is asking.

2. Decide whether you need a 'Terms of Reference' section. If you do, write it now.

3. Define the scope of your report.

4. Decide whether you need a 'Scope' section. If you do, write it now.

5. Decide whether you need an 'Introduction' section. If you do, write it now.

6. Decide whether you need a 'Method' section. If you do, write it now.

7. Referring to your scope, write down the principal section headings.

8. Against each section heading write down roughly how many words or pages you intend to produce, taking into account any word count limit. If you are writing the report in a group, assign sections to each of the group members (see Figure 7.3).

Figure 7.3   Group report structure

1. TERMS OF REFERENCE   (150) — Jane
2. SCOPE   (150) — Rav
3. INTRODUCTION   (200) — Chris
4. STRATEGY   (2000)

    4.1. Market sector   (600) — Rav
    4.2. Finance   (500) — Jane
    4.3 Sales strategy   (900) — Angel

If you are writing a group report pick one person to make sure it all hangs together – a sort of report coordinator.

9. If necessary, break each section down into subsections and possibly subsections within these (see Figure 7.4).

Figure 7.4   Group report with sub-sections

1. TERMS OF REFERENCE   (150) — Jane
2. SCOPE   (150) — Rav
3. INTRODUCTION   (200) — Chris
4. STRATEGY   (2000)

    4.1 Market sector   (600) — Rav
    4.2. Finance   (500) — Jane
    4.3. Sales strategy   (900) — Angel

      4.3.1. Sales staff   (600)
      4.3.2. Commission rates   (150)
      4.3.3. Sales reports   (150)

You now have the basic structure of your report. It might change as you go on it but at least you have a starting point. To complete the report, continue with the following steps:

1. Decide the position of any pictures, diagrams, tables, graphs and so on that you might want to include.

2. Write the sections of your report making reference to any appendices you might need.

3. Produce any appendices you have included.

4. Decide whether you need a 'Conclusions' or 'Recommendations' section. If you do, write them in now.

5. Read your report and try to reduce the number of words as much as possible.

6. Proofread your report or, better still, ask a friend to proofread it for you.

Make friends with a good English student and ask them to proofread your reports.

7. Number the pages.

8. Decide whether you need a table of contents. If you do, write it in now.

9. Produce the front cover.

And there you have it!

WORD PROCESSORS

On many HE courses you will have to use a word processor to produce your assignments and, in some cases, word processing will be part of your course. However, it's very unlikely that you will be taught the advanced features of these systems. Virtually all HE institutions will provide you with access to powerful word processors. Learning their advanced features will probably take one or two weeks of solid work, depending on your previous experience and how familiar you are with computers. This might sound like a lot, but it will be time well spent for the following reasons:

- You will save a great deal of time in the long run.
- You will get higher marks for your work.
- You will have learned a valuable skill which is highly prized in the job market.

Don't make the mistake of thinking that word processing is only for typists and secretaries. If you do, you will become one of a dying breed – everyone should learn how to use a word processor if they want to advance in their career. So let's see just why learning these advanced features will save you time and get you marks.

Proofing tools

Most people know that word processors can check and correct your spelling mistakes, but they can also correct a range of other typing errors such as duplicate words and omitted capital letters after full stops.

Most systems include an 'on-line' thesaurus that can be very useful for finding those elusive words.

The more advanced systems have grammar checkers to help you with sentence construction. Some can be 'tuned' for particular writing styles, business reports, dissertations, letters, and so on. The very advanced ones even include fog counters which tell you how easy your work is to read. We used one to help write this book!

Document templates

Document templates, sometimes called style sheets or master documents, are special documents that store standard presentation styles and document layouts. Modern systems have a library of these documents specifically designed for reports, dissertations, letters, presentations, and the like. You can call up these templates and use them as a basis for your work. Alternatively, you can modify them to meet your own requirements or even design new ones from scratch.

Document outliners

Document outliners are sometimes known as document profilers. They are powerful tools which help you design and manage document structures. Amongst other things, they can automatically number sections in a report and generate a table of contents at the touch of a button!

Graphics

Modern word processors have a whole range of facilities for adding graphics and will include a library of 'clip art' that you can use to enhance your work.

Headers and footers

Word processors can put the title of your report in the header of every page and also number your pages automatically.

There are many different word processors on the market; most of them come in the form of software which can be run on a personal computer. The latest products are 'windows' based, that is, they have a 'graphical user interface' and are designed to work with a 'mouse'. Try to learn one of these windows based systems. As well as being more modern, they are also more powerful and easier to use.

Don't be afraid to explore the system; you won't break it.

Don't just read textbooks on word processors; the only way to learn is by using them!

Most systems have a series of on-line tutorials to help you learn them. You will usually find these in the 'Help' menu.

If you ever think to yourself, 'I wish it could do ...', it probably can. Use the 'Help' facility to find out how.

If you are going to use floppy disks to store your work, always use two of them. They are notorious for getting corrupted, and have a particular aversion to rain, beer and being carried around in coat pockets. If you are ever tempted to back up your work on only one 'floppy', remember this story:

It's 10.45 on the evening before you have to hand in an important assignment. You have just finished, and it's a masterpiece. You back up your work on to a 'floppy' and rush off down to the Student's Union just in time for a last drink with your friends, safe in the knowledge that all you have to do is print off your report and hand it in the next day. Morning arrives, and suddenly you are staring in horror at 'Unrecoverable disk error on drive A' written across the middle of the screen. 'If only I'd made two copies, it would only have taken another minute,' you cry. You ask your tutor for an extension and she's sympathetic, giving you a one-day extension and agreeing to knock off only one grade. You work flat out for the next 12 hours and end up with a 'C'.

People who make this mistake only ever do it once. Try not to make it at all – make two copies every time.

8 PROJECTS

Projects will usually form a significant part of your course, so make them count. Final-year projects are especially important. As we have mentioned before, if, at the end of your course, you are on the borderline between two classifications, your project grade might well be used to decide whether you go up or down. It's also likely that potential employers will be very interested in what you did for your final-year project and what grade you recieved.

CHOOSING A TOPIC

One of the worst mistakes you can make with project work is to get the first step wrong – choosing the right topic. When you are selecting a topic make sure the answer to all these questions is 'yes':

- Am I interested in the topic?
- Will it be easy to obtain information about the topic?
- Is there plenty of opportunity to do some practical work?
- Can I immediately see how the theory I've been taught might be relevant?
- Do I think the project will be interesting to the employers I'd like to work for?

PLANNING A PROJECT

You will get more than enough time to complete projects – usually between six and eight months. This might sound like a long time in October, but by April you might start to panic if you have done no work. Common sense tells you to start your project early. Starting sooner rather than later helps you in many ways:

- You can do most of the work before getting bogged down with finals revision.

- Your project won't be rushed and badly presented.
- You will be able to see your tutor without too much competition from other students.
- There will be less demand for library books and articles.

PRACTICAL WORK

Don't make your projects too descriptive; try to do some practical work wherever possible, as opposed to just consulting the library. This will both make your project more interesting to read and help demonstrate its application to the real world – in other words, it will win you more marks. Furthermore, doing something practical will probably also make your project more enjoyable. Here are some ideas for practical work:

- Interview people to get ideas, opinions and facts.
- Conduct a small survey.
- Watch people to see how they behave.
- Conduct an experiment.
- Do some voluntary work which is related to your project.

Try speaking to people in shops, but remember to get permission from the shop management.

Don't do postal surveys if you can help it; the return rates will probably be very low and they can be quite expensive.

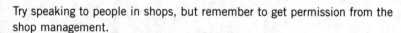

Persuade some of your friends to help you do an experiment.

RELATING TO THEORY

Many students struggle to relate their projects to the theory taught on their course, but it's essential that you do this. There will probably be a marking criterion called something like 'relation to theory'! You will have less of a problem in relating your project to theory if you have already learned to apply the material taught on your course. To relate theory to your project you must systematically examine your research and try to match areas of it to the specific subjects you have studied.

Use a different coloured pen to mark areas of your research. Use the colours as a code to reflect which subject each part of your research is related to:

- Marketing   (red)
- Human Resource Management   (blue)
- Finance   (green)
- IT   (orange)

Once you have matched the research to the subjects re-examine your course notes and ask yourself the following questions:

- Does my research support any particular theories?
- Does my research support one theory more than another?
- Can I use any of the analysis tools I have been taught to help me understand my research?
- Is the theory helpful in explaining my results?

CONCLUSIONS

You should always have a 'Conclusions' section in a project report. Make sure that the conclusions you reach bear an obvious relation to the content of the project – don't introduce anything new.

Include a number of conclusions that talk about your own educational experience. Say what you think you have learned and how it's helped your development as a student. You can't fail to get some marks for this, and there may even be a marking criterion specifically for it!

REPORT STRUCTURE

For all the reasons we explained earlier in Chapter 7, make sure that your report is well structured.

When structuring project reports bear these questions in mind:

1. Why was the topic of interest in the first place?

2. What did I set out to do?

3. What did I do?

4. What problems did I have?

5. What were the results?

6. How do my results relate to academic theories?

7. How do I interpret the results of my work – opinions, conclusions, and do I have suggestions for further work?

8. What have I learned?

9. How have I developed?

If you can answer these questions you will be able to produce a well structured and interesting project report. In many cases, you will even be able to base your main section headings on these questions.

COMMON MISTAKES

There are numerous mistakes you can make on a project, but most bad projects can be traced back to one or more of these basic errors:

- picking the wrong topic in the first place
- starting late
- inadequate planning
- budgeting insufficient time
- careless reading of the regulations and requirements
- failing to meet the project supervisor soon enough
- failing to listen carefully to the project supervisor's advice
- having a poor report structure
- lack of practical work
- too much description
- lack of relation to theory
- failing to describe all the work done
- insufficient opinion and argument around the topic
- lack of evidence to support arguments

9 PRESENTATIONS

You will often have to submit your assignments and projects in the form of presentations as well as reports – a prospect which fills many students with a sense of dread. If you are one of them, don't worry, help is on its way. Before we go into detail let's demolish a couple of myths about presentations:

Myth: Some people just can't do presentations. They either become too nervous or too embarrassed.

Fact: If they use the correct techniques everyone can become a competent presenter.

Myth: Reading a presentation from 'cue cards' or preparing a speech will be both helpful to you and impress the tutors.

Fact: Cue cards and speeches will ensure a poor presentation.

WHAT IS A PRESENTATION?

Presentations sell something! Commercial presentations usually sell a product or service. Student presentations generally sell the results of an assignment or project. As in any sales situation, it's the way that you sell that counts – the product you are selling is not as important as you may think!

Copying tutors

Many students think that the way to do presentations is to copy the way tutors do lectures. But, though tutors might offer you some advice about presentations – and you should always take note of any preferences they have – contrary to what you may think, most lectures are excellent examples of bad presentation technique! This is for two reasons. First, most tutors are bad presenters; they will have had little or no training in presentation skills, unlike presenters in a commercial environment. Second, as you will see later, delivering a high quality presentation requires a great deal of concentration and effort. Most tutors can't maintain such a high standard of delivery day in, day out. You might think 'but surely if I do the same as the tutors they will be impressed and flattered?'. This is not so; most tutors don't realize just how poorly presented their lectures are – if they did, they'd probably do something about it. If you copy a tutor's presentation technique they may well mark you down for the very same mistakes they themselves make on a regular basis!

Image

Most students think that presentations are simply for conveying factual information, but that's only half of it. Presentations also convey an image which is determined by a number of subtle factors such as:

- terminology
- voice intonation
- dress
- body language
- the visual attractiveness of your presentation (your OHP slides and the like)

It is possible to present exactly the same information with different images. For instance, you might want to present one image to a group of fellow students and a totally different one to your professor. Professional presenters are able to modify their image to fit the audience they are presenting to. The degree to which you can modify your image will depend on your personality and previous experience of presentations. You can present a dramatic, humorous or serious image under different conditions. However, a boring image is not recommended! There is no right or wrong image for HE presentations; it depends on the particular circumstances. The important thing is that your image has been planned.

Ask the tutor what style of presentation they like. They might not be able to tell you but it's worth a try. But bear in mind that it's your presentation. Don't attempt a style that's likely to be a problem for you. For instance, if the tutor responds to your question with 'I like to see a bit of humour' but humour is not your strong point, don't try it.

MARKING OF PRESENTATIONS

Presentations will be assessed by either tutors or, in the case of 'peer group assessment', your fellow students. In either case there will usually be a marking criterion for 'presentation technique'. This generally has a weighting of between 10 and 25 per cent, but the real weighting for presentation technique will probably be much greater. Let's see why.

Marks for selling

As with report assessments, when a tutor experiences a good presentation they will subconsciously be more generous with marks for other criteria. Imagine two sales professionals trying to sell the same car. The good sales professional succeeds where a poor one fails because, although the product is the same, the customer perceives it as being better! The same applies to presentations. Think of your audience as the customer – the content of your presentation will appear better if you make a good sales pitch. The science of selling is complex, but one of its basic principles is that people's buying criteria are generally ranked in the following order:

1. the person they are buying from

2. the organization they are buying from

3. the product that they are buying

If we convert this priority list into one for HE presentations it looks like this:

1. your image

2. your group's image (if it's a group presentation)

3. the content of your presentation

Makes you think, doesn't it?

Extra marks for content

As you will see later, one of the key objectives of a presentation is to hold the audience's attention. If you present something but don't have the audience's attention then you didn't present it! As far as the audience is concerned, it never happened. This is not the audience's fault. People automatically switch off if they are bored or unimpressed.

You put a diagram on the OHP but the audience can't understand it because the labels are too small. The tutor asks you to read the labels and explain the diagram. You put up another OHP slide with the same fault and, again, the tutor asks for an explanation. You put up a third slide but, this time, the tutor doesn't ask anything – he's bored and has switched off. No information was presented on the third slide – you might as well not have bothered producing it in the first place! Sadly for you, this slide contained the results of some excellent research. But, as far as the tutor is concerned, you never did this research and therefore you don't get any marks for it! Most tutors will try to concentrate on your presentations much more than their commercial counterparts, but there are limits!

COMMON SECTIONS

In Chapter 7 we discussed the common sections you might find in a report (pages 73–96), emphasizing strongly that there are no sections that have to be included in **every** report. The converse is true for presentations. Because presentations are designed to sell something, and selling is a very structured process, you will normally need most of the following sections if you want to deliver a good presentation.

Introduction

You should always be introduced. If you are giving a presentation on your own you should introduce yourself. The purpose of an introduction is:

- to tell the audience your name
- to give the audience a brief overview of the topics you will be presenting
- to establish your credibility to talk about these topics

In some professional presentations introductions can take quite a while but, for you, about 20 seconds will usually suffice.

If you are doing a group presentation you should introduce the speaker who follows you and the first person should give a brief introduction to the presentation as a whole. Don't introduce all the group members at the beginning – the audience won't remember them all.

If you are not introducing yourself you need to know exactly what your introducer will say – every single word! This avoids two common problems that often spoil the beginnings of presentations. The first problem is the introducer telling the audience information that's wrong. Getting your name wrong is quite common, and saying that you will be covering areas that you won't be is even more common. In extreme cases the audience can be told something that's totally false or even embarrassing. This means that, during your opening statement, you may have to contradict what your introducer has said – not recommended for good grades! The second problem occurs when the introducer covers ground that you intended to cover in your opening statement – in other words 'steals your thunder'. This means that you either have to change your opening statement or repeat what your introducer said.

When you are planning a group presentation make sure all the introductions are agreed at the planning stage – then agree not to change them!

Establishing your credibility to cover a topic is very important. You are much more likely to sell the content of your presentation to the audience if they think you know something about it. If you have some previous experience that you can use to establish your credibility, use it. Never think that you have little or no credibility to talk in a HE presentation – because it's not true. The research that you have done always gives you some credibility. Consider the following examples of introductions:

'Good afternoon everyone. My name is Jane Good-Student, and our group will be covering the marketing strategy for Clever Co. PLC's export drive. I will now hand you over to Dawn Bright-Student who'll be taking you through our literature survey. Dawn was chosen for this task because she used to work as a librarian.'

'Good afternoon everyone. My name is Jane Good-Student, and our group will be covering the marketing strategy for Clever Co. PLC's export drive. I will now hand you over to Dawn Bright-Student who'll be taking you through our literature survey. Dawn's been speaking to John Verybright, the Marketing Manager of Bright Marketing Ltd, to find out his view as to what literature we should use.'

'Good afternoon everyone. My name is Jane Good-Student, and our group will be covering the marketing strategy for Clever Co. PLC's export drive. I will now hand you over to Dawn Bright-Student who will be taking you through our literature survey. Dawn has spent several weeks looking at this issue and therefore can only give you a summary of her findings.'

Opening statement

Trying to plan exactly what you will say for an entire presentation – that is writing a speech – is a bad idea as you will see later. But, like introductions, opening statements should be planned down to the last word. Knowing your opening statement will help for a number of reasons:

- It will give you the confidence to begin to talk.
- It reduces the possibility of being lost for words.
- The opening statement sets the scene for what you are going to say.

Opening statements should have **impact.** They should immediately seize the audience's attention.

Make your opening statement one of the following:

- **A joke.** But remember that bad jokes are bad news. Test your joke before the presentation to make sure people find it funny.
- **A rhetorical question.** This will make the audience think and ensure you have their attention.
- **A profound statement.**

Objectives

The objectives section of a presentation is similar to the 'Terms of Reference' section in a report. It's important to let the audience know what your objectives are because you will want the markers to assess you against your own objectives rather than any preconceptions they might have about your presentation. Let's consider this example assignment:

Using the attached case study (Clever Co. PLC), prepare a 15 minute presentation on which areas of the market you think Clever Co. PLC should target for its export drive *(group exercise).*

Here is an objectives section you might use for this assignment:

'Our objectives for this presentation are to:

- demonstrate that we have read and understood three methods by which a market can be segmented
- demonstrate the research methods we used to identify these segmentation techniques
- produce evidence that we have selected the most appropriate segmentation methods for Clever Co. PLC
- provide a detailed description of the market segment we are recommending for Clever Co. PLC
- gain feedback from you as to your views on our analysis'

Agenda

An agenda is a list of the main topics that your presentation will cover. If you are doing a group presentation you should write the name, or at least initials, of the person who will cover each topic (see Figure 9.1). Unless you are told otherwise, the last item on the agenda should always be a questions section.

Figure 9.1   Presentation agenda

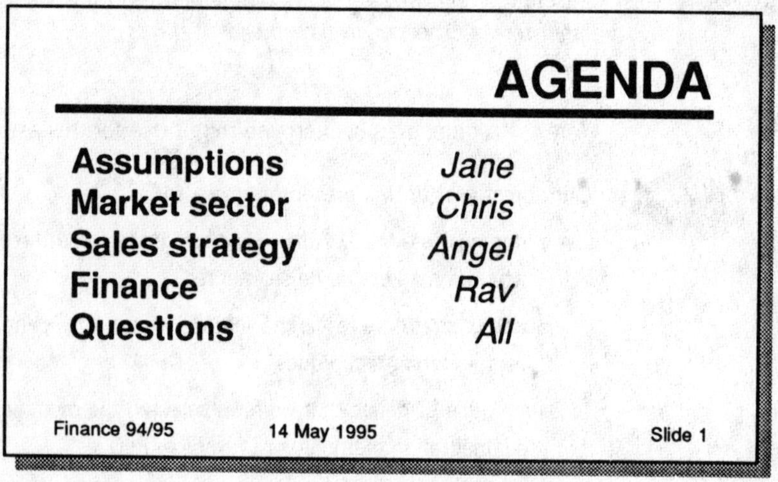

AGENDA

Assumptions	*Jane*
Market sector	*Chris*
Sales strategy	*Angel*
Finance	*Rav*
Questions	*All*

Finance 94/95   14 May 1995   Slide 1

Scope

The scope section of a presentation has the same function as that of a report. The objectives and agenda might well imply a scope but, sometimes, you will want to draw the audience's attention to any specific issues that relate to the scope of your research.

Method, procedure, approach

As with reports, a method, procedure or approach section tells your audience how you did your research. In the case of presentations it's sometimes useful to tell them how you put the presentation together and why you selected the image you did.

Assumptions

If your presentation relies on any assumptions which won't become obvious during its course, it's a good idea to state them at the beginning.

'Before we get into the main part of our presentation I'd like to say that I'm assuming everyone has read our preliminary report on Clever Co. PLC.'

Body

The body of your presentation contains all your findings. It should take your audience through a logical and structured progression that will lead them to agree with any conclusions or recommendations you will be making at the end of your presentation.

Conclusions and recommendations

In line with the sales philosophy of presentations, your conclusions and recommendations should be grouped together at the end. The idea is that, by this time, the audience will be prepared to believe anything you say!

'In conclusion, ladies and gentlemen, we believe that Clever Co. PLC would meet little or no resistance to introducing the proposed IT system as long as they follow these recommendations:

One, fully brief all staff on the nature of the new IT system and why you need it.

Two, get the views and ideas of all staff concerned.

Three, include at least two members of operational staff on the project team.

Four, consult the Unions before making changes to any working practices.

A virtually identical system was successfully implemented at Smart Co. PLC where similar recommendations were followed.'

Closing statement

Closing statements are extremely important and also need to be planned word for word. A closing statement should generally contain the following four items in this order:

1. a reference to how you have met the presentation objectives. (Refer to each objective, stating how you have dealt with each of them.)

2. a profound statement that leaves the audience with something to think about

3. a note of thanks to the audience for their time and attention

4. an invitation to ask questions

'In summary, I'd like to demonstrate how we have met the objectives for our presentation. I will now put up the original slide that stated our objectives. Hopefully you can see that we have:

- demonstrated that we have read and understood three methods by which a market can be segmented

- demonstrated the research methods we used to identify these segmentation techniques

- produced evidence that we have selected the most appropriate segmentation methods for Clever Co. PLC

- provided a detailed description of the market segment we are recommending for Clever Co. PLC.

Our final objective was to get some feedback, and I will come to that in just a moment.

Before we did this assignment we thought that marketing was easy but, to be honest, we struggled. We now know that segmenting a market is a complex task that needs to be approached methodically. We are obviously not experts yet, but I think we have come a long way!

Finally, I'd like to thank you for your time and address that last objective by inviting you to ask us some questions about our presentation.'

PRESENTATION MEDIA

You can use many different types of visual media in a presentation including:

- OHPs
- whiteboards
- flipcharts
- videos
- video cameras
- computer-generated images
- 35mm slide projectors

In this book we will only be dealing with OHPs, flipcharts and whiteboards, because they are commonly available in HE institutions, but many of the principles we will be describing apply to all media.

USING OVERHEAD PROJECTORS

We will now explore some of the issues related to preparation of OHP media.

Styles and templates

Like reports, OHP slides should have a consistent and aesthetically pleasing style that matches the image you want to present. It's worth spending some time designing a good style and then using it over and over again. Figure 9.2 shows an example.

Figure 9.2   Example of an OHP slide style

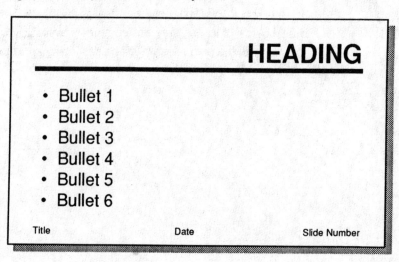

Check the type of OHPs that are used in your HE institution. Some of them won't project the entire contents of an A4 slide. Many presentations have failed because the slides didn't fit on the OHP! When designing OHP slides it's a good idea to take an A4 piece of paper and draw a 40mm border around the inside of it and place it underneath your slide. Make sure nothing that you write or draw on the slide goes outside this border.

You can create 'template slides' with borders and logos by doing a design on a piece of A4 paper and photocopying it on to transparencies. Make sure you use the right type of transparencies for this – some will melt in a photocopier!

Pictures and diagrams

A picture is worth a thousand words. Use as many pictures and diagrams as possible and reduce the amount of text in your presentation to an absolute minimum. This will help you maximize the limited time you have available.

Text

Any text that you do use should be as large as possible. In an average-sized classroom or lecture theatre most people can't read text smaller than 18 points in size. To be on the safe side try to use text that's no smaller than 24 point.

This is 18 point text

This is 24 point text

Bullets

Most text in presentations should be shown as a list of bullet points that relate to the points you want to make. Bullet points aren't self-contained explanations intended for the audience to read; they are 'cues', which act as triggers for **you** to start talking about particular points or topics. They also act as reference points to help the audience keep pace with your presentation.

Try to make your bullet points brief – a single word if possible and never more than two lines.

After you have written a bullet point read it back to yourself. Try to make its meaning obvious **only to you**. If this is not the case, simplify it – you will see why later.

Don't put more than six bullet points on an OHP slide.

Don't put full stops after bullet points. They aren't sentences.

Emphasis

As in reports, you might want to emphasize certain words or points on an OHP slide. You can use the same techniques, such as boldening, underlining or capitalization.

Use dark grey for 'normal' text and 'bold black' for emphasis. This is a particularly good trick if you are writing your OHP slides by hand.

- This is a normal bullet point

- This a bullet point with an **emphasized** word

- **This is a very important bullet point**

Colour

If you are going to use colour in your slides be careful! It's very easy to make OHP slides look over-complex and unattractive by using too many colours.

Limit the number of colours you use to three or four. Try using one colour for bullet points, another for text and another for emphasized text.

Colour is great for emphasizing points, but most people choose red for this. Red looks great on paper and computer screens but often becomes 'washed out' when projected on an OHP. Use bright green or turquoise instead.

Numbering

For long presentations, number the slides so that you can replace them in the right order if they get mixed up – for instance, if you drop them on the floor five minutes before you start your presentation!

PRESENTATION SOFTWARE

Most HE institutions will provide you with access to software that is specifically designed for producing and delivering presentations. Most such programs are easy to learn, and you can become competent in as little as half a day, depending on your previous experience. But, like modern word processors, most of them also have the advanced features we described in Chapter 7 (pages 94–96). The message here is the same as for word processing: the better you are able to use this technology the more time you will save and the more marks you will get.

Remember, the best styles are the simple ones. OHP slides should be clear and effective, not masterpieces of graphic art!

Limit the number of fonts you use to **one.**

Use a simple font like 'Helvetica'. This will make your slides easier to read.

USING FLIPCHARTS AND WHITEBOARDS

Flipcharts and whiteboards are some of the most dynamic media available. You can produce very exciting presentations with them and they are excellent for explaining unpredicted questions. Unfortunately flipcharts and whiteboards are probably the hardest media to use well.

Writing and drawing

One of the problems with using flipcharts and whiteboards in unforeseen circumstances is that the audience has to wait while you are writing or drawing. If you know that you intend to use a flipchart or whiteboard, draw or write anything you will need before the presentation begins. Anything you do have to draw or write during the presentation must be done as fast as possible in order not to lose the audience's attention.

Write as fast as you can and say the words out loud as you write them. It's not necessary to write neatly because you are telling the audience what it says as you go along. In other words, the text is just a cue.

Figure 9.3   Write fast

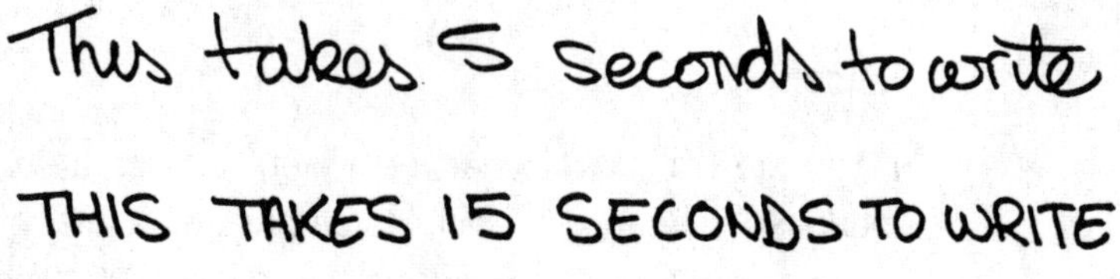

This takes 5 seconds to write

THIS TAKES 15 SECONDS TO WRITE

The trick for fast drawing is basically the same as for writing. Draw something that is understandable when the audience have been told what it is. It's disastrous to spend ages drawing pictures and diagrams; it's amazing what you can get away with. Take a look at these two cars – you only know the first one is a car because we have told you!

Figure 9.4   Draw fast. (This takes 5 seconds)

Figure 9.5   Draw slow. (This takes 60 seconds)

Colour

If you are using a flipchart or whiteboard use a selection of coloured markers. You can use colour to emphasize points, but you should also change colour occasionally just to add interest. The different colours don't need to relate to anything in particular.

When you are drawing or writing on a flipchart hold a selection of markers in your non-drawing hand. This will remind you to change colour occasionally and also allow you to make a quick change if a marker runs out.

PREPARING A PRESENTATION

There is a saying amongst professional presenters, 'Preparation prevents poor performance' and it's right! Careful planning will help you avoid many pitfalls. As with reports, you should plan your presentation structure before you do any research. Here's how you might answer an assignment that requires a presentation.

1. Take a sheet of paper and write the title 'Objectives' at the top. Underneath it, write down your presentation objectives.

2. Define the scope of your presentation.

3. Decide whether you need a 'Scope' section. If you do, take another sheet of paper and write the title 'Scope' followed by a list of bullet points that summarizes the scope of your presentation.

4. Referring to your objectives and scope, write down, on separate sheets, the titles of the main sections you want to include in your presentation.

5. If you are delivering a group presentation write the name of the person responsible for each section on the appropriate sheet.

As with reports, if it's a group assignment, pick one person to coordinate it.

6. If necessary, break down each section into subsections just as in a report.

7. Write down how many minutes you intend to talk on each of your sections or subsections (see Figure 9.6).

Figure 9.6   Rough presentation design

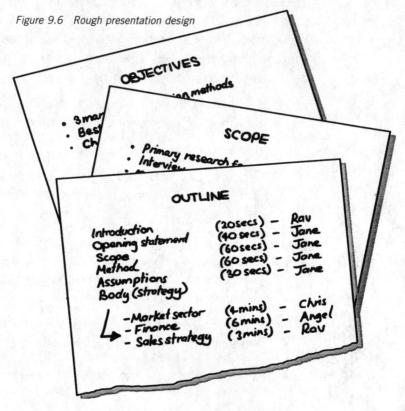

The time it will take you to present a single OHP slide depends on many factors, but an average slide will take two or three minutes to present.

Allow at least two minutes at the end for questions.

8. Do the necessary research for your sections and subsections.

When you are researching a topic think about how much time has been allowed for it in the presentation. There is no point doing more research than you can fit in.

9. On the appropriate sheets write a list of bullet points and sketch any diagrams and pictures that represent the results of your research.

10. Decide whether you need a 'Method' or 'Approach' section. If you do, take another sheet and write the title 'Method' or 'Approach' at the top followed by a bullet list that summarizes the method or approach you used to research your presentation.

11. Decide whether you need a 'Recommendations' section. If you do, take another sheet of paper and write the title 'Recommendations' at the top followed (you've guessed it) by a list of bullet points summarizing your recommendations.

12. Decide whether you need a 'Conclusions' section. If you do, take a sheet of paper and write the title 'Conclusions' at the top then write down a list of bullet points that summarizes your conclusions. This can be added later if you are not yet able to decide on them.

13. If it's a fairly long presentation, write an agenda.

14. If it's a group presentation, get together and make sure that each group member reads everyone else's slides. This will ensure you understand each other's part of the presentation. If necessary, make any adjustments to ensure the presentation hangs together correctly.

15. If it's a group presentation, agree all the introductions.

16. If it's a group presentation, agree a standard format for any OHP slides you need, preferably by using a standard template.

17. Produce any OHP slides you need.

18. Number the OHP slides.

And there you have it!

PRESENTATION STRESS

Many people experience extreme stress giving presentations. If you are one of them, it's essential to deal with stress in order to get good marks.

What is stress?

Most stress is caused by a perfectly normal response to fear. So, what is fear and why do we experience it? In his famous book, *Dune,* Frank Herbert said 'Fear is the mind-killer'. But fear can be both good and bad. Fear is a basic and essential human mechanism that helps keep us alive, protecting us from dangers that can harm or kill us. Without fear we would all be quite willing to crawl along narrow window ledges of high buildings. As we grow older, our experience teaches us to fear more and more things and at the same time, we also tend to become more fearful of things that we haven't come across before.

How does fear affect us?

Humans have an automatic, and normally beneficial, reaction to fear. This is best explained by a well known principle known as 'fight or flight' that relates to our caveman ancestors. Cavemen were constantly threatened by dangers, such as rival tribes, wild animals and raging fires, so they developed an elaborate mechanism for dealing with them – fight or flight.

A caveman sees a hungry sabre-toothed tiger running towards him. He has two options, either to stand and fight, or attempt to escape (the flight option). Whichever he chooses, a number of complex physical and mental changes would be automatically triggered to help him:

- His heart rate would be increased to its maximum level in order to supply more oxygen to the muscles in his body. This would help him either escape as fast as possible or increase his strength for fighting.

- Large quantities of adrenaline would be released. This would increase his strength and power output for a short time during the early stages of the flight or flight.

- The blood supply to the parts of the brain specializing in 'high level' functions, such as creative thinking, would be redirected to those responsible for physical activities.

This is an extreme example of a response to fear where virtually all the caveman's mental and physical resources have been dedicated to a single objective – staying alive for the next few minutes. No real thought will be given to pacing himself nor would he feel any pain if the tiger mauled the back of his legs. Both the nature of the threat and the individual's personality will determine the degree of their response to fear. Less threatening situations, like crossing a fast river, might have stimulated a similar, but less extreme, response. Similarly, a more laid-back caveman might not be too fazed by the sight of a sabre-toothed tiger.

So, what has all this got to do with presentations? This answer is; 'Quite a lot.' Modern humans react no differently than cavemen to fear; it's just that the nature of the threats has changed. We aren't likely to stumble across any hungry sabre-toothed tigers nowadays, but a presentation might seem just as frightening. Threats don't have to be physical – in fact, most of them aren't. So how do we handle non-physical threats? In exactly the same way!

Why are presentations threatening?

The following are some of the threats posed by the prospect of giving a presentation:

- getting a poor grade
- embarrassing yourself in front of your tutors
- embarrassing yourself in front of your friends

The fear of losing friendship can be particularly serious. What your friends think of you affects both your personal and academic life. You might think that giving a poor presentation in front of them is going to lead to a loss of popularity or being branded as a wally. Even professional presenters have been known to crack up in front of their peers.

It's five minutes before a peer group assessed presentation and you are frightened. Your heart beats faster than usual and your awareness is strangely heightened because of the adrenaline in your body. You get stomach pains because the stress is causing an imbalance in your body fluids and you feel like going to the toilet every couple of minutes. You start to pace round because your body is trying to burn up some of the adrenaline and extra oxygen you have produced. The presentation starts and you can't remember what to say, you can't even think straight, yet you are fully aware of the faint ringing of a phone in the next room. You become aware that you are shaking slightly and think to yourself, 'This is going to be a disaster!'.

The extent to which this situation applies to you will vary. We all respond to stress in different ways and to different degrees. Some people can stay relaxed in the face of anything life throws at them, whilst others experience 'panic attacks' when confronted with a presentation.

Dealing with fear

Our experiences in life teach us to be afraid of certain things. Usually this helps us. For instance, learning not to put your hand in fires is a big help. But, at some points in our lives, we all learn to fear things that can't actually do us a lot of harm. The good news is that you can unlearn these irrational fears, the bad news is that sometimes it can take time. Fear is conquered through understanding. Let's see how.

When people feel stressed they immediately become aware of its symptoms. This in turn leads to even more stress until some people reach 'overload'. Understanding the nature of stress and knowing the symptoms it causes will help you break this vicious circle. Understanding what stress is, and how it affects you, will cause you less stress when you experience an irrational fear.

It's important to understand the nature and implications of the threats that cause you stress. If you are threatened by a hungry sabre-toothed tiger it's a good idea to experience fear, but presentations aren't quite so dangerous. Consider this hypothetical conversation.

Student: What if I crack up and forget what to say in my presentation? Surely I will fail or get a bad grade?

Answer: Very unlikely; most audiences, and particularly tutors, will be very sympathetic and help you to recover from mistakes. It's possible to make quite a lot of mistakes without losing too many marks.

Student: OK then, but suppose I really do make a mess of it and fail, what then?

Answer: You will almost certainly be given another chance. Remember, too, that a single presentation will probably have a pretty minimal effect, overall.

If you haven't been told already, ask your tutor what would happen if you failed at your first attempt – they will be happy to tell you. Ask in a professional and direct way, as if you are asking for a set of facts, not reassurance – you don't want to give the tutor the impression that you think you might fail. Ask as far before your presentation as possible, giving the tutor plenty of time to forget that you even asked the question at all.

Student: That's fine, but all my friends will be there. They will laugh at me if it goes wrong.

Answer: Real friends will share a laugh with you but none of them will laugh **at** you – they will probably offer you some encouragement or advice. If they do laugh at you, then they weren't your friends in the first place!

Of course you should make every effort to give good presentations, and it's both natural and desirable to feel some stress, but try to keep things in perspective.

You also need to know how to combat the effects of stress directly. This is a complex medical area which we can't tackle in detail, but here are a couple of tricks that you might like to try out:

Run as fast as you can for about 30 seconds, two to three minutes before your presentation begins. Running on the spot in the toilet will do fine. This will burn up some of the oxygen and adrenaline you might have produced and will help calm you down.

If you know you suffer from stress associated with activities such as giving presentations, read some books on stress management.

The final weapon you need to combat fear is self-confidence. For instance, many experienced rock climbers feel quite relaxed while walking on narrow ledges of high buildings. They don't get too frightened because they have learned that they can do it – their experience has taught them not to be frightened. By the end of this chapter you will have learned how to be a competent presenter. And, of course, the more presentations you give the better you will become. You might even end up enjoying them.

Not enough stress

As you become more competent at giving presentations you might begin to suffer from a problem which professional presenters often experience – not enough stress! If you ever feel tired or hung-over beforehand, you might need to psych yourself up a bit. There are various techniques for this. Rugby players, for example, usually perform some form of ritual such as counting out loud combined with running on the spot.

Run as fast as you can for about 30 seconds. Do this two to three minutes before your presentation begins. Running on the spot in the toilet will do fine. That's right – it's the same trick as for 'too much stress'. It works both ways; the running will help wake you up!

DELIVERING A PRESENTATION

Now, let's talk about how you go about delivering a good presentation.

Set up and preparation

Remember, 'Proper preparation prevents poor performance'. Follow this procedure before all your presentations.

1. Make sure all the equipment you will need will be in the room. For instance, if you need a video don't assume that the tutor has read your mind and organized one for you. Similarly, don't assume that if a piece of equipment was there last week it will be there next week; equipment gets moved around at lot in HE institutions.

2. Make sure you know how to use all the equipment. Trying to show a video clip when you don't know how to turn on the video recorder is very tricky!

3. Have a flipchart or whiteboard available even if you don't plan to use them. Of course, you will also need some marker pens and maybe something with which to clean the whiteboard.

Buy markers designed for whiteboards. It's very embarrassing trying to wipe indelible writing off a whiteboard! Whiteboard markers work on flipcharts as well as whiteboards.

4. If possible, go into the room at least 10 minutes before your presentation starts and make sure you have the following items with you:

- a selection of coloured marker pens for use with the flipchart or whiteboard

- two pens

- a notepad

- a wristwatch or small clock

- any slides you intend to use, prepared in the correct sequence

- any notes you intend to use

- a 'pointing device'

5. Arrange the seating in the room.

6. If you are using slides, put one on the OHP and switch it on. As well as making sure that the OHP works, this will give you the opportunity to set it up correctly. Doing this after you have started your presentation is both unprofessional and a waste of time!

Set up the OHP using a test slide with a pleasing picture and the word 'WELCOME' at the top. Leave the slide in place so that the audience sees it as they arrive.

7. Put your notes and wristwatch in a discreet place where they aren't visible to the audience (you will see why later).

8. Put your pens and notepad where they are visible to the audience – show them that you are prepared.

Sequence

The sequence of events in presentations varies, but try this for a start.

1. Introduce the presentation.

2. State the objectives of the presentation.

3. If you are using an OHP or flipchart ask the audience if they can see it clearly. Of course, they should be able to because you will be well prepared, but you never know, you might have missed something. If there are any problems, solve them. This might involve asking people to move – no problem, just ask and they will do it.

4. State the agenda for the presentation.

5. Ask the audience if there is anything they want to add to the agenda. If they say 'yes', write it down on your notepad.

6. Tell the audience they are free to interrupt and ask questions at any time.

Many students insist on saying something like 'Would the audience please leave any questions until the end?' Professional presenters do the opposite, for several reasons. First, it's impolite – you are effectively telling the audience to shut up! Second, it's essential to tackle issues raised by the audience as they arise, since the audience member will probably have forgotten their question by the end of the presentation. Third, if a member of the audience is left wondering about some issue, you lose their full attention. Questions also make the presentation more interactive and interesting (see pages 144–145).

7. Introduce the first speaker.

8. Make the opening statement.

9. Deliver the presentation.

10. Deal with any items the audience might have added to the agenda. If you are presenting in a group, take a few seconds to decide who'll deal with them.

11. Make the closing statement.

After the presentation, clean the whiteboard and rip any pages you used out of the flipchart. This will prevent any students presenting after you stealing your ideas!

Using overhead projectors

Using OHPs is simple, but most people still manage to get it wrong. We have already discussed how to prepare OHP slides and set up an OHP (see pages 116–119), so now let's see how you actually use them.

You need to highlight the points you are making with some sort of pointing device. There are numerous objects you can use, from old car aerials to 'laser wands'. Highlight items on the projection screen rather than the projector itself, otherwise you will probably end up blocking someone's view. When you are pointing, make sure you look at the audience and not the screen – talking with your back to people is bad manners.

Many people will advise you to use 'cover sheets' to unveil information on OHP slides, but don't believe them.

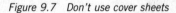
Figure 9.7   Don't use cover sheets

Professional presenters never use cover sheets because they have some serious drawbacks. First, the piece of paper or card tends to fall off the OHP when you reach the bottom of the slide. Second, you have to stand very near to the OHP to use them, which will probably result in you blocking someone's view, as well as preventing you moving around and getting amongst the audience. Third, research has shown that, when presented with a partially covered OHP slide most people will spend the first few seconds wondering what is hidden beneath it. Again, if the audience is left wondering, you haven't got their attention, and when you haven't got their attention you can't score any marks!

People who use cover sheets will tell you that they stop the audience reading ahead and are therefore essential for holding the audience's attention and for getting them to focus on the particular point you are making. These people are trying to solve the wrong problem. The real problem is to stop the audience reading ahead without using a cover sheet. There are two ways of doing this. First, you can use a sequence of 'overlay slides' which give the effect of adding information to the same OHP (see Figure 9.8).

Figure 9.8   Overlay slides

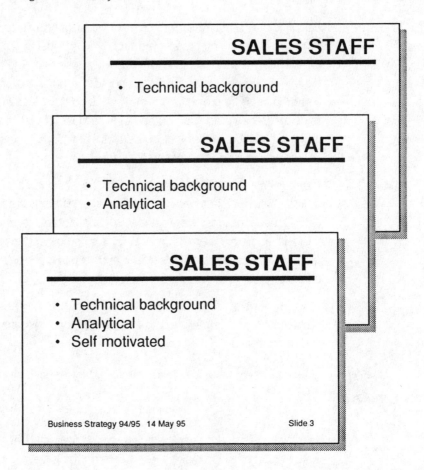

Second, you can use well designed bullet points as we have previously suggested. Good bullet points mean little or nothing to the audience without you talking around them. If you put a well designed slide on the OHP and count to three – the amount of time it takes to read six short bullet points, you will then have the audience's full attention.

Finally, remember to switch the OHP off when you are not using it. Leaving it switched on when you are not using it is just another distraction.

Timing

Failing to use all the available time wastes the opportunity to score marks. Similarly, overrunning the allowed time limit and being cut short by the tutor is also disastrous, since you don't just lose marks for presentation technique, you also lose marks for content. Running over time is very common in group presentations and you need to make sure this doesn't happen. Because the most important sections – that is conclusions, recommendations and the closing statement – usually come at the end of the presentation, it's a big marks loser.

Rehearsing is the only real way to find out how long it will take you to give a presentation. Unfortunately, we all speak at different speeds according to the amount of stress we are under, so it's preferable to rehearse in front of a trial audience, perhaps made up of some of your friends. This will make the rehearsal far more realistic and help you gauge the time more accurately.

Most audiences' attention span is 20 minutes. If you are doing a presentation that is designed to take longer than this, introduce some sort of brief break.

The break might be as simple as pouring a drink or handing out some literature.

As it's very easy to lose track of time during a presentation, glance at your watch occasionally to make sure you are on the pace.

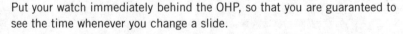

Put your watch immediately behind the OHP, so that you are guaranteed to see the time whenever you change a slide.

Get someone in the presentation audience to warn you, with a discreet cough for instance, if you are off the pace. Of course, this is very easy in group presentations because you can warn each other.

Notes

Using notes reduces your interaction with the audience. Keep the use of notes to a minimum and never use cue cards. Contrary to popular belief, reading from cue cards or reading speeches will increase the chances of losing your way in a presentation. This is because synchronizing cue cards with OHP slides is very difficult.

In some cases you might need some notes but, in most cases, the information on the slides or other media will be sufficient if you have a good understanding of what you are presenting.

As we have said before, it's tempting to look at the OHP screen when you are talking to the audience. This is natural as you also need to see what's on the slides. You can avoid this by using the following trick.

Copy your slides on to some paper to use as notes. You can fit six slides on to one side of an A4 sheet. Place these immediately behind the projector so that you can read them while you are looking at the audience (see Figure 9.9). By the way, presentation software can produce these sheets automatically!

Figure 9.9   Using notes

Audience interaction

As we have said a few times already, a good presentation should involve the audience. Professional presentations involve the audience about once every minute. But what is audience involvement exactly? It's any activity that encourages the audience to 'do something'. Here are a few ideas for involving the audience:

- Ask them questions.
- Ask them rhetorical questions.
- Ask them to raise their hand if they agree with something.
- Ask them to think about something you have said.
- Give them something to look at, such as a handout.

When planning a presentation, include some specific actions for involving the audience. If necessary, include these 'involvement points' in your notes.

Making eye contact is an essential part of interacting with the audience. Try to scan the audience from side to side if they are sitting in a single row or in a zigzag pattern if they are in a number of rows (see Figure 9.10).

Figure 9.10   Audience scanning

Varying the intonation in your voice will also help you hold the audience's attention. Unless you do it naturally, it's very difficult to maintain an interesting flow of speech, but you should at least be able to emphasize the important points.

Speak louder when you come to points or words that are written in bold on your OHP slides.

Body movement

Body movement generally comes in two forms, the good and the bad (there is also the ugly!). Good body movements include:

- gesturing with your hands when emphasizing important points
- walking among the audience while you are speaking

On the other hand, bad body movements include:

- pacing round in a circle
- swaying from side to side
- repeatedly pulling the top on and off marker pens
- swivelling from side to side whilst sitting
- jingling keys or coins in your pocket
- playing with your wristwatch
- repetitive scratching in the crotch region (the ugly!)

Most of us will do one or more of these in presentations, but unfortunately we don't realize it because nobody ever tells us. Similarly, many people have an annoying habit of repeating words or phrases over and over again.

Ask people to tell you if you do things like this – and don't get upset when they tell you!

Take everything out of your pockets before the presentation starts.

Put pens down when you are not using them.

Don't put your hands in your pockets.

Again, get someone in the presentation audience to send you a discreet signal if you are 'doing it'.

Questions

Questions are a very important part of presentations. Tutors will ask you questions for a number of reasons:

- They haven't understood what you have said.
- They disagree with what you have said and are asking you to confirm your view.
- They are testing your understanding of the issues surrounding your presentation.
- They are testing your question-handling technique!

When you answer questions remember the four-stage LIAC procedure:

1. **Listen.** Listen to the entire question. Never interrupt the questioner no matter how slow and boring they are. Interrupting a questioner and trying to pre-empt the question is a bad idea for two reasons. First, it's impolite. Second, you might pre-empt it incorrectly and end up answering the 'wrong' question. Presentations aren't quiz shows.

2. **Interpret.** Unless the meaning of a question is obvious, such as 'Did you enjoy doing this presentation?', you will have to correctly interpret questions before answering them because some questions can be ambiguous.

'How much do Clever Co. PLC sell each year?'

This question is meaningless, since you don't know whether the questioner is asking for sales by volume of cash, or sales by volume of products, or perhaps something completely different. There are two likely consequences of answering a question like this straightaway. First, you might fail the tutor's test on question-handling technique. Second, you might answer the wrong question. A good response to this question would be something like 'Would you like to know Clever Co. PLC's sales by volume of cash, value of products, or some other measure?'.

3. **Answer.** Next, you should answer the question as best and as honestly as you can. If you don't know the answer, say something like, 'I don't know. Can I find out and get back to you in the next couple of days?' Make sure that you **do** get back to the tutor with an answer; don't assume that they will forget about it. Never lie. The tutor will probably know or suspect that you are lying even if they don't reveal at the time that they have caught you out.

4. **Confirm.** Finally, confirm that you have given a satisfactory answer by asking something like, 'Has that answered your question?'. If you receive a negative response ask the questioner to explain their question in more detail.

As we said earlier, it is a good idea to allow the audience to interrupt your presentation with questions. But this does present a problem – in that someone in the audience might ask you a question relating to something you intend to cover later. If you are asked a question that you think pre-empts your presentation say something like 'I think your question will be answered later in the presentation. Please tell me at the end if it hasn't been covered' and then write the question down on your notepad. At the end of the presentation ask the questioner to confirm that their question was answered.

Attitude

You should approach presentations with a positive attitude. It's your presentation and you are in control.

Professional presenters don't apologize for mistakes; you will rarely hear a DJ or TV presenter do so. Apologizing will both undermine your credibility and encourage the audience to dwell on the mistake rather than focus on what you have to say next. But you should never ignore mistakes even if you think the audience might not have noticed – it's more than likely that they did!

Make a joke out of the mistake, perhaps by blaming it on someone else in a lighthearted way.

Just explain what happened to cause the mistake.

Suppose you put up an OHP slide and notice that you have made a spelling mistake. You could turn to the audience and say something like 'OK, who's spotted the spelling mistake? It's a good job I'm not on an English course'. This will work even if you **are** on an English course!

Stalls

A stall is when you lose your train of thought and forget what to say next. It happens to everyone from time to time, so don't worry if it happens to you. Here's the three-stage process to go through if you stall.

1. **Think.** If you stall, you will know immediately, but it will take the audience about three seconds to detect a problem. Spend this time thinking about what you want to say next rather than worrying about the fact that you have stalled. Often, these few seconds will be enough for you to remember what you want to say, and you can carry on without the audience even noticing a problem.

2. **Recap.** If, after three or four seconds, you are still stuck, recap on the important points you have covered before, perhaps referring to the bullet points on your slides. This helps in three ways:

   - It buys you some time

   - It emphasizes the main points of your presentation

   - It can very often be the trigger you need to regain your train of thought

3. **Take a time out.** If you still can't remember what to say, take a 'time out', preferably using a dash of humour. Say something like 'I've completely forgotten what to say. Just talk amongst yourselves for a while'. After you have fully regained your composure and train of thought recall the audience's attention by saying something like 'OK, are you are ready for round two, everyone?'.

10 EXAMS

The first thing to decide about exams is when to do them! In most HE institutions – particularly modular institutions – you will be given a fairly wide range of options to choose from in order to make up your course. Different options will almost certainly have different assessment strategies. In other words, some will have exams at the end of the course whilst others may be based entirely on continuous assessment. Find out how your options are assessed before making your selection.

Assessment strategies are quite often published in subject or course guides. Try to obtain these guides from the course administrators rather than attempt to track down the relevant tutors. This will generally be far less time-consuming and stressful!

Don't automatically shy away from exams just because they make you nervous – this can be a big mistake. Exams make most people nervous and you may be better at exams than you are at continuous assessment. Try to assess objectively how good you are at exams, and remember that it's your performance relative to the other students that counts.

Think about the exams you have done in the past and how well you did compared to others – you might be surprised!

If you know that exams aren't your strong point, concentrate on options that use continuous assessment.

REVISION TECHNIQUES

If you do any revision you might like to start by rereading some sections of this book – use the 'trix' we showed you in Chapter 3.

What is revision?

To revise something means to see it again after an initial acquaintance. Many students have problems with revision because they are, in fact, seeing a subject for the first time! True revision is only possible if you have studied a subject conscientiously throughout your course. Curiously, while nobody expects to fly an aeroplane or drive a car within a few hours, some students expect to learn complex subjects the night before an exam. There are no short cuts.

Effective revision

You need to budget your revision time according to your ability in particular subjects. Aim to minimize the damage in your weak subjects as well as maximizing your performance in your strong ones. It's very tempting to allocate more revision time to your strong subjects, but you will probably achieve a better overall grade by focusing on the bad ones. Similarly, don't ignore any subjects completely. Your priority should be:

1. the subjects you must pass in order to complete your course

2. your weak subjects

3. your strong subjects

Intensive revision

Some students are tempted to revise in a frenetic burst leading right up to the exams, sometimes using stimulants like caffeine tablets or even illegal drugs to keep them awake and alert. This only works for a minority of students who can tolerate a high level of physical and emotional stress and may even thrive on the pressure. But even these students won't be able to keep this up for long.

For most students, intensive revision should be avoided if possible. In our experience, most students are better off doing a moderate amount of revision and reaching the examination room rested and relaxed. Similarly, don't do last-minute revision, such as reading a book outside the examination room – it generates stress. It is more beneficial spending your time trying to relax.

The revision plan

You need to make a revision plan, and stick to it. A good plan is based on repeating cycles, whereby you revise each subject several times. With each cycle you make your notes shorter and shorter until you eventually 'boil down' the subject to two sides of A4 at the most. Reducing a subject to its essential principles like this will not only produce you a good set of revision notes, it will also give you a good understanding of the subject.

Here is an idealized revision plan based on the following assumptions:

- you are studying six subjects (S1, S2, S3, S4, S5, S6) all of which have an exam
- you are equally good at all of them
- you have two exams on each of the 10, 11 and 12 June

Of course you will need to adapt this plan for your particular circumstances and study strengths, but it's a good start.

Revision Blocks	1 June	2 June	3 June	4 June	5 June	6 June	7 June	8 June	9 June
2 Hrs	S1	S2	S3	S4	S5	S6	S1	S4	S1, S2
2 Hrs	S1	S2	S3	S4	S5	S6	S2	S5	S3, S4
2 Hrs	S1	S2	S3	S4	S5	S6	S3	S6	S5, S6
	Cycle 1						Cycle 2		Cycle 3

This plan gives each subject a total of nine hours' revision, split into three cycles. The days are divided into 'revision blocks' of two hours each. Try to break the blocks up with meals and domestic chores; if possible, try to take some physical exercise as well. Remember, you won't be capable of effective revision for very long stretches at a time.

Try to take a small break of about five minutes every time you complete 20 minutes of revision. Do the washing up, tidy a drawer or watch an episode of *The Magic Roundabout*.

CLOSED BOOK EXAMS

In a closed book exam you aren't allowed to use any documentation that's not provided to you in the exam. You will be working without reference documentation – that is, you will need to remember all the relevant knowledge and be confident in your ability to apply it. Closed book exams terrify some students for precisely this reason; they see them as memory tests.

A test of memory

The extent to which closed book exams test your memory will vary between subjects and the tutors setting the exam. But, unlike school exams, it's extremely unlikely that HE exams will concentrate on the recall of facts. Most questions will tell you the facts and then test your understanding and ability to apply them.

When you are revising for closed book exams you need to cover the core knowledge and skills and their *application*. Don't concentrate too much on trying to remember all the facts unless you know that you will need them.

Question prediction

Many students become obsessed with what topics will come up and try to do selective revision, sometimes known as question-guessing or question-spotting. Selective revision might work if you are lucky, but it's very risky; the chances are that you will eventually come across an exam paper where none of 'your' topics come up.

Read all the paper

A common problem is that a student spots a question containing a familiar topic and proceeds to answer it without reading all the paper first. There are several reasons why you shouldn't do this. First, you might have read only part of the question. Second, there might be a better question later on in the paper. A common example of this is the numerically-oriented question with a small descriptive section at the end.

In a finance exam you are asked to 'Prepare a cost benefit analysis for the attached case study'. You know you have good numeric skills and leap into the production of a model answer. Then you spot 'Part B' over the page that asks you to 'Discuss a number of non-numeric methods that could be used to appraise the study' – and you aren't so good at this!

OPEN BOOK EXAMS

Students commonly think that open book exams are easy – they aren't! You need to revise just as much for open book exams as you do for closed book ones.

Preparation

Prepare for open book exams in exactly the same way as you do for closed ones. The books, notes and reference material taken into the examination room should be there to provide you with back-up; they are not a means of learning the subject during the exam.

Case study questions

You might be given a case study to analyse before the open book exam. This can be difficult. If you have had a week or so to prepare an analysis of the case study you will be expected to give very comprehensive answers to any questions about it.

Don't attempt to write out a model answer to the question that you think will be set and then simply copy it out in the exam. You don't know what the question will be. A better approach is as follows:

1. Thoroughly read the case study. Make sure you understand it and that there are no confusing errors or ambiguities.

2. Try to obtain some relevant reference material. For example, if it's a business case study, search out some information about similar companies in the real world.

3. Use some analysis tools that you think can be applied to the case. For example, a business studies student might choose to prepare a SWOT analysis.

The remainder of your preparation should be as for a closed book exam. Remember, there is no substitute for thoroughly knowing the subject.

MULTIPLE CHOICE QUESTIONS

Unlike some of the other questions we have discussed, multiple choice questions are often concerned with facts and very basic principles.

Organizing and remembering

Use some of the techniques we described in Chapter 3 (pages 13-40) to organize relevant knowledge and commit it to memory. For example, if you are using a mind map or knowledge tree, practise so that you can recall it and draw it out at will. You will be surprised how easy it gets after a while – try it with some old exam papers.

Working out the answer

Sometimes you can work out the answers to many multiple choice questions by using a combination of common sense, fundamental knowledge and the information given to you in the answer choices. Even if you can't work out the answer entirely you can often narrow down the number of sensible answers to two or three at the most.

IBM is the largest computer company in the world with an annual turnover of around:

1. $60 000

2. $6 000 000

3. $60 000 000

4. $60 000 000 000

5. $60 000 000 000 000

A simple 'feel' for business sizes will lead you to the conclusion that the first three figures are far too low. Similarly, the last one is far too high to be the turnover of a single company. In other words, a basic knowledge of business, rather than a specific knowledge of this company, can lead you to the right answer.

If you don't know the answer to a multiple choice question, and the paper makes no mention of marks being deducted for wrong answers, always have a guess. There is a reasonable chance that you will be right, and you have nothing to lose!

SELF-PREPARATION

It's natural to panic before exams. If you are facing an exam right now and feeling a bit panicky read pages 126–131 – it might calm you down a little.

You should aim to enter the examination room in a calm and confident state of mind. You can help yourself by completing your revision the day before the exam and getting a good night's sleep.

You might have your own methods for getting to sleep but here are a few ideas:

- Take some vigorous exercise, such as playing a game of squash.
- Have a modest amount of alcohol but don't get drunk – a hangover will do you no good at all!
- Don't use sleeping tablets unless you have been prescribed them by a doctor.
- Don't use illegal drugs – they will almost certainly do more harm than good.

Aim to arrive at the examination room 10 to 15 minutes before the exam is due to start – don't give yourself time to wait around getting wound up. If it's an afternoon exam, have a relaxing lunch followed by a short walk.

TIME MANAGEMENT AND OPTIMIZATION

Timing is critical in exams. To achieve maximum marks you must answer all the necessary questions.

Most exams will tell you how many marks are awarded for each question, and you should allocate time accordingly. If no marks are stated, assume that all questions are worth the same.

Aim to complete all the questions in around 85 per cent of the available time, thereby leaving you time to review your answers and complete any parts you may have missed.

In the age of word processors many students find it hard to write quickly and legibly. Practise your handwriting before your exams. This will not only enable you to write faster, it will also probably gain you a better grade – presentation is also important in exams.

AFTER THE EXAM

Forget it! There is nothing you can do to influence the outcome of an exam once you have walked out of the room. Worrying about it won't do you any good and might adversely influence your preparation for any following exams. However, on rare occasions, you may feel that you were personally disadvantaged by conditions in the exam room – perhaps by a group of rowdy students who weren't removed by the invigilators, or an error in the exam paper that you didn't notice until the end. If you think your performance was significantly affected by something like this, you should complain in writing immediately after the exam.

Most HE institutions will have some sort of Appeals Officer who will help you with the procedure.

11 VIVAS

Vivas are exams in which you are interviewed by a number of tutors. Usually you are personally invited to attend vivas, and it's always a good idea to accept the invitation because, as you will see, failure to do so might result in you failing your entire course! The most common reason for tutors to invite you to a viva are:

- to decide whether your grade should go up or down if you are on the borderline between two classifications, particularly if you are in the 'pass–fail' zone

- to help tutors mark your project

- to decide whether or not the grade you get for a group assignment should be awarded on an individual basis

Think of vivas as a selling opportunity – you are there to impress the tutors and you have nothing to lose. They will probably make any changes to your grades immediately after the viva so you must leave them with a good impression. Remember, people buy from people – make sure the tutors buy what you are selling.

Here's what you should do if you get invited to a viva:

1. If you know that you are being examined on a particular piece of work, read it thoroughly the night before and prepare a one-minute summary of it in your head.

2. If a tutor offers to go through your work with you before the viva, accept their offer immediatly and pay attention to any suggestions they have.

3. Be punctual.

4. Look organized. Have any appropriate work to hand so that you don't have to rummage for it in your briefcase or bag.

5. Show interest when you are talking about your work.

6. Give the tutors your full attention.

ANSWERING QUESTIONS

You need to be good at answering questions in vivas. As with most assessments in HE, the questions will be probably be open, so it's very important to listen carefully and note how they are phrased.

If you don't understand a question, politely ask the tutors to explain it to you.

If you need time to think about a question say something like, 'That's a difficult question. Can I have a little time to think about it please?' – they will agree!

A common type of question asked in vivas is the 'summarize' question. Suppose you are in a viva which is being held to support a project. If a tutor asks you to summarize your work, never say something like 'It's all in the report' because in effect, you imply that they have not read it. Give them the one-minute summary you prepared the night before.

Another common type of question is the 'we are surprised...' question. If a tutor says something like 'I'm rather surprised you did that. Didn't you consider...?', they are really saying, 'I think you did it the wrong way, and the way I'm suggesting would have been better'. A question like this demands two responses. First, explain why you carried out the task in the way you did and why it seemed like a good idea at the time. Second, say something like 'I think your way of doing things would have been better and I will keep it in mind for the future'. Tutors don't expect you to be as good as they are, and flattery will get you everywhere!

The basic rule to remember when answering questions in vivas is to emphasize what you have learned. Always make sure that tutors are aware of any mitigating circumstances that might have prevented you from doing a better job, but don't whinge – tutors have problems too.

12 THE LAST TRICK IN THE BOOK

This chapter is very important because the issue under consideration is **you!**

AT THE BEGINNING OF YOUR COURSE

If you are at the beginning of your course you may wish to consider this.

For most people the time spent in HE will have a major impact on shaping the rest of their lives. This is true in both a personal as well as professional sense; indeed, it is difficult to separate the two. So let us consider briefly how your approach to HE might effect **your** career and **your** future life.

The world economy is both complex and dynamic, but you may have noticed a number of underlying trends:

- the number of students graduating from HE is rising
- their average grades are improving
- the number of jobs for which they are competing is falling!

Differentiating yourself from other graduates in the job market is becoming increasingly difficult. There are already well qualified and experience people from most professions on the dole. Competing with them will be difficult. In short, unless you are one of the small minority who are exceptionally talented or just plain lucky, life for you outside HE will be hard enough as it is without making it any harder. It is vital, therefore, that you make the best use of the opportunity that has been placed before you. By this, we don't just mean studying hard; it is important that you explore your new environment to the full and profit from the 'HE experience' as much as you can. You will learn as much outside the lecture theatres and classrooms as you will inside them. Join clubs, talk to students on other courses, find out what the libraries and computer centres have to offer you – most of it will be free. Remember, HE is about **education** not training for work – most students will end up in jobs which aren't directly related to their course. Whatever you choose to do with your time, don't waste it!

AT THE END OF YOUR COURSE

If you are now at the end of your course, and there seems to be nobody around who is offering to give you a large sum of money out of the kindness of their hearts, you have two options; stay on in HE, or enter the job market. In either case we invite you to consider these three questions.

1. Where will the big career opportunities be in three to five years time?

You need to look this far ahead because for most graduates this is the time when they are beginning to mature in their careers. Of course, the precise timing will depend on the particular graduate and career concerned, but for most people this is about right.

There is no point gearing yourself up for a 'dying profession'. If you are like most graduates you will want to pursue an area of the job market that is either fairly stable or, preferably, growing. If you can successfully identify and position yourself within an area that reaches peak growth in that three-to-five-year time frame it is likely that you will be very popular with employers. For instance, graduates of the early 1980s who gained employment in the IT and Pharmaceutical industries tended to enjoy very prosperous careers. Their roles varied from sales executives to particle physicists, but the one constant was their high salaries! There will be new opportunities in the coming years – find out what they are by:

- keeping abreast of current affairs
- exploring a wide range of industries
- talking to as many successful people as you can

2. What are my strengths?

Try to think objectively about what differentiates you from other graduates. What abilities do you have that many of them haven't? These may be specific 'industry skills'; for instance, you may, during your course, have become an expert on a specialist piece of software used for forecasting company profits. Often your final year project will have given you some industry specific skills. Alternatively you may have developed a strong set of 'transferable skills' which could be applied to a range of industries. Perhaps you have become an accomplished presenter or technical writer. It may even be that you have developed highly prized non-academic skills – HE has produced quite a few explorers, professional sportspeople and rock stars in its time!

We are all special in some way. Try to match your strengths to your career aspirations.

3. What are my interests?

This is the most important question of all. We hope that by this time your interests are closely related to your strengths. If this isn't the case, do something about it right now!

When making any major decision that effects your career it is essential that you seek the highest degree of long-term job satisfaction possible. Most people spend a large proportion of their waking hours at work. It may be that you are forced to take a boring job which simply pays the bills for a while, but don't get stuck in a rut, move on as soon as you can. If you wake up in 20 years time dreading the thought of another day at the office and recalling how you always wanted to be an Officer in the Navy, it may be that you have only yourself to blame. Of course, we all have to accept that there are limits to the opportunities available, but most people have more options than they think. Don't assume that any doors are closed before you have tried them.

Now we will leave you with the last trick in the book – good luck.

Spend **your** time pursuing those goals which will keep you happy and fulfilled!